Rehousing

# Peter Friedl
# *Rehousing*

*Sternberg Press*

This book is published on the occasion of the exhibition
"Peter Friedl: Teatro" at Kunsthalle Wien (March 22–June 9, 2019).

Editor: Kunsthalle Wien
Managing Editors: Vanessa Joan Müller, Eleanor Taylor
Translations: Thomas Cooper (Attila Bartis), William M. Hutchins (Ibrahim al-Koni), Silvester Mazzarella (Davide Longo), Megan McDowell (Mike Wilson), Jeffrey Zuckerman (Céline Minard)
Photos: Jorit Aust
Copyeditor: Eleanor Taylor
Design: Vladimir Llovet Casademont
Printing: Medienfabrik Wien – Graz

ISBN 978-3-95679-551-0



Distributed by The MIT Press, Art Data, and Les presses du réel

Sternberg Press
Caroline Schneider
Karl-Marx-Allee 78
D-10243 Berlin
www.sternberg-press.com

# Contents

# Foreword

## *Vanessa Joan Müller*

*Rehousing* is, first and foremost, the title of a series of ongoing works which Peter Friedl began in 2012. The *Rehousing* series comprises a selection of individual, intricate, and true-to-scale models of houses. Each structure reproduced in minute detail was chosen by the artist primarily due to its historical, social, and political significance. One is purely autobiographical. Collectively, the structures materialize as constructed environments that reflect the recent past, different biographies, and ideologies in diverse ways; they are, in Friedl's words "case studies for the mental geography of an alternative modernity."

All models are presented as equal in a stripped back, neutral manner. Always on display atop minimal, plinth-like square tables with thin steel legs, the architectural model can be viewed just below eye level, where minute features appear when at arm's length. Windows can be peered into, while balconies, terraces, brickwork, and graffiti, emerge as well defined on closer inspection.

The models of *Rehousing* carry numerous readings. However, extracted from their multiple inscriptions only allusions to their specific sites and stories are conveyed. The titles provide clues, yet beyond their local context, what the structures signify is an approach to residing and living driven by ideologies, rarely by utopias. The models within *Rehousing* often present themselves as ruins, failures, or the manifestation of highly asymmetrical distributions of power.

The laconic title "Rehousing" is reminiscent of initiatives aimed at combating homelessness with social and urban prevention strategies, such as the "Homelessness Prevention and Rapid Re-Housing Program," introduced by the US Department of Housing and Urban Development in 2009. In view of the unemployment figures in America after the financial crisis in 2008, the program's political significance outweighed the lasting practical effects. Nonetheless, it shows how political agency manifests itself in questions of living.

*Rehousing* is also the title given to the present publication, which revisits and reconceives the series through the juxtaposition of images of the individual models with a diverse collection of short stories and poems. Imagined as an anthology, as well as an artist book, it constitutes a reframing of the houses by the contributing authors—each of whom have submitted a text that either expands on the separate history of the buildings, draws on them to realize alternative fictions, or departs entirely from the origins of the related house altogether. *Rehousing* furthermore signals a change of location: a literal or (perhaps, more prominently even) metaphorical move to another type of accommodation, space, place, shelter, or home.

Models provide new ways of thinking and looking at things. The concept of the model as an abstract, concentrated form representing reality or projecting a potential future, plays a fundamental role in Friedl's artistic practice. His multifaceted projects—heterogeneous in terms of medium, style, and meaning—are invariably interpreted as models: as exemplary articulations and solutions to aesthetic problems.

In pursuit of new narrative models, his work explores the construction and limits of representation, employing conceptual strategies such as permanent displacement, contextual transfers, critical intimacy, and the reinterpretation of genres left over from the history of modernism.

Within the *Rehousing* series, the idea of an international modernity designed by renowned architects is countered with anonymous, in some cases, bricolage-like dwellings in which the complex repercussions of this expansive project "modernity" can be traced to the present. The politically motivated need for representation is confronted with evidence of displacement and colonization, individual concepts with standardized forms, and local building traditions with modernist aesthetics. Each model stands alone. However, as with all models, the possibility of comparison is vital to their understanding.

The exhibition *Teatro* at Kunsthalle Wien addressed several recurring themes in Friedl's œuvre: the concept of the model, language, translation, and theatricality. The publication project, developed on the occasion of the exhibition, brings *Rehousing* into focus, and the individual works it is composed of, two of them presented in Vienna for the first time. Two larger architectural models that relate to the series (*German Village* and *Tripoli*) were also exhibited in *Teatro*, and feature within this publication. Regardless of their size, Friedl's choice to include them is founded on their essential proximity to the others.

The concept was to invite a variety of voices to respond to the *Rehousing* project, taking one architectural model as a starting—or vanishing—point for narration. Left entirely open to the invention of the individual authors, the contributors imaginatively engaged with the proposal to submit a text or poem in relation to a specific architectural structure, and, by extension, approached this model house with their own literary constructions. They meditated and reflected on the images of the models provided, realized alternative perspectives, and reinvented stories that—in some cases—stray far from the original context of the building in question. While some contributions bear no direct correlation, others touch at the heart of the situated context and complex of interconnections that the particular house in question presents.

*Gründbergstraße 22* is named after the street and number of Friedl's Austrian childhood home. Mark Z. Danielewski and Céline Minard each contribute their own personal takes on *Gründbergstraße 22*. Danielewski opens doors and windows into time and place, breathing life into "the house." Minard's fictional piece, in contrast, transports the reader together with her six-year-old protagonist on a ray of light to the moon. Ann Cotten makes "Some Architectural Considerations" in relation to a traditional stilt house structure based on Ho Chi Minh's private residence in Hanoi. Karen Pinkus addresses *Villa tropicale*, a never-realized residential building designed by Luigi Piccinato for East Africa in the 1930s. She imagines the villa "as a model for a stage set." Dionne Brand and Hanif Abdurraqib chose Evergreen, a model of one of the slave huts built at the Evergreen plantation established in Louisiana in the eighteenth century. Davide Longo's contribution relates to *Heidegger*—a replica of philosopher Martin Heidegger's wooden cabin in the Black Forest mountains of southern Germany. For Heidegger, language was "the house of Being." Longo's short and pointed text explores perceptions of being, death, grief, and suffering. Mark von Schlegell, in "D. Nomen," takes *Oranienplatz* as a point of departure for his "book of death" horror story. The model depicts one of the shacks built by African refugees requesting political asylum in Berlin and taken down by the police in 2014. Amina Cain's text is inspired by *German Village*, a scaled-down model of the two-story residential housing unit established in an army compound in the middle of the desert in Utah. Drafted by Erich Mendelssohn and Konrad Wachsman and constructed in 1943, the mock village combined urban architecture of the Rhineland and Berlin. It was built for testing firebombs developed for Allied airstrikes on civilian targets.

*Tripoli* is the model-sized realization of a sketch made in 1931 by Italian architects Carlo Enrico Rava and Sebastiano Larco for a branch of the Fiat car company in Tripoli, Libya. The *razionalismo* style characterizes many of the colonial buildings in North and East Africa during the Italian Fascist era. Ibrahim al-Koni's contribution is comprised of excerpts from his not yet translated 2006 novel: *Min Makan Naskunu, Fi Zaman Yaskununa (In a Space We Inhabit, in a Time that Inhabits Us)*. Set in Tripoli during the Qaramanli Dynasty, which ruled Tripolitania between 1711–1835 CE, the scenes portray a new nineteenth-century ruler trying to negotiate with the French Ambassador, and in conversation with his Sufi gardener. *101* refers to the one hundred identical houses built between 1965–67 for the employees of the national bank of Cambodia in Tuk Thia, Phnom Penh. Designed by Vann Molyvann, it demonstrates the combination of traditional Khmer architecture with modern sensibilities, bringing the design concepts of Le Corbusier to Cambodia. Attila Bartis and Mike Wilson contributed in relation to this model of residential housing. Wilson's short story charts the tale of Roque, an elderly man, and a dog, "who showed up on his own, big and black with a blue tongue." Bartis employs the form of a "mockup" to wryly imagine the family lives of "One Hundred Government Clerks." Annemarie Jacir and Hala Alyan poetically approach *Azraq*. A case study in contemporary political architecture, *Azraq* portrays a container house from a refugee camp in Jordan. Jacir's poem is emotive, rich with colors, and Alyan's piece, "Interactive Fiction :: Windows" takes a form she calls "coetics," as an intersection between computer coding and poetry wherein the reader determines how the poem progresses. Renee Gladman and Nalo Hopkinson chose *Dome* for their contributions. The domed structure—inspired by Buckminster Fuller's geodesic construction principles—is a replica from the hippie commune Drop City which was founded in South Colorado in 1965 and abandoned in the mid-1970s. Gladman's "Untitled (Euclidean) for Peter Friedl's Dome" looks at "dome living," while Hopkinson's science-fiction tale unravels the story of a woman and an artist case-worker. Madeleine Thien's text "Holdout 198" developed from *Holdout*, a so-called "nail house" or *dingzihu*—representing one of many resistant local structures which defied the Chinese building boom. Thien visits and converses with her mother in the apartment where she had grown up. *8115 Vilakazi Street* is a model of the former home of Winnie and Nelson Mandela, in Soweto, South Africa, now transformed into a museum. Achmat Dangor and Mohale Mashigo look at the small red brick house through the eyes of young protagonists; Dangor's "Koelie" kids, and Mashigo's Thandi. Addressing the "fabled rainbow nation," Mashigo's piece orbits on Thandi's observations, while Dangor's story follows the path of two brothers walking home.

Finally, Sabrina Orah Mark's contribution departs from *Amona*, which is based on one of the prefabricated houses of the Israeli outpost called "Amona." Located on Palestinian territories on the West Bank, the settlement was demolished in 2017. Orah Mark's story tells of two sons who "leave on a bus the color of figs to fight in the Gentle War."

To our minds—our "*houses* of thought"—the overarching title *Rehousing* might suggest a mental remapping. The prefix "re" often serves to connote a return to something, to recapture, or look back. The prefix "re" may also indicate repetition, to repeat, designate "again," or "again in a different way," such as signifying something as rewritten or renewed. Following this line of thought, the book *Peter Friedl: Rehousing* binds together a reconfiguration of the series it is named after—the (hi)stories of the houses are here rewritten.

* * *

We wish to thank each and every one of the authors for their enthusiasm, vigor, and energy, in realizing such imaginative, beautiful, tender, and touching contributions.

Our thanks also go to the translators for taking on the delicate and decisive task of translating these inventive works of contemporary literature.

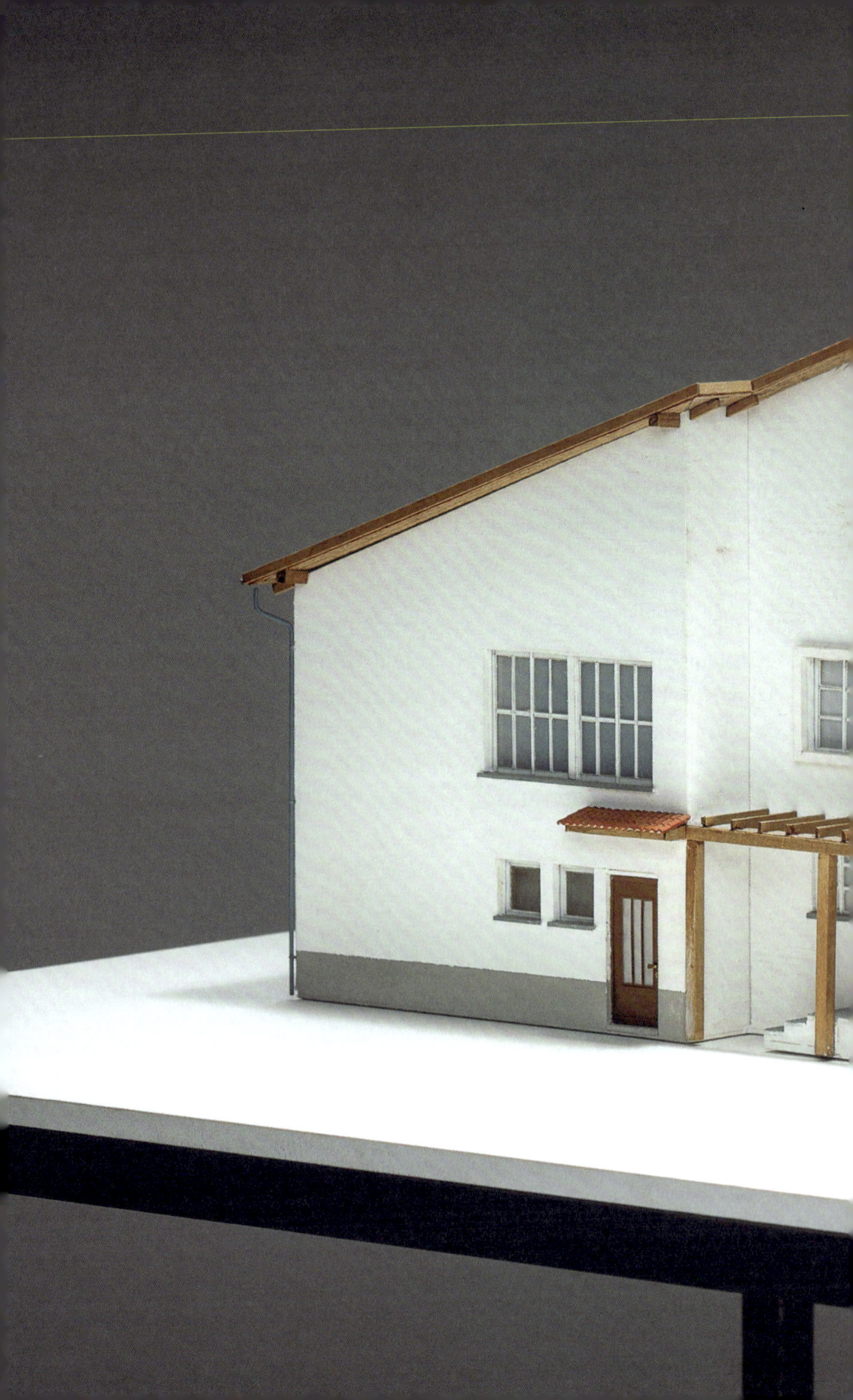

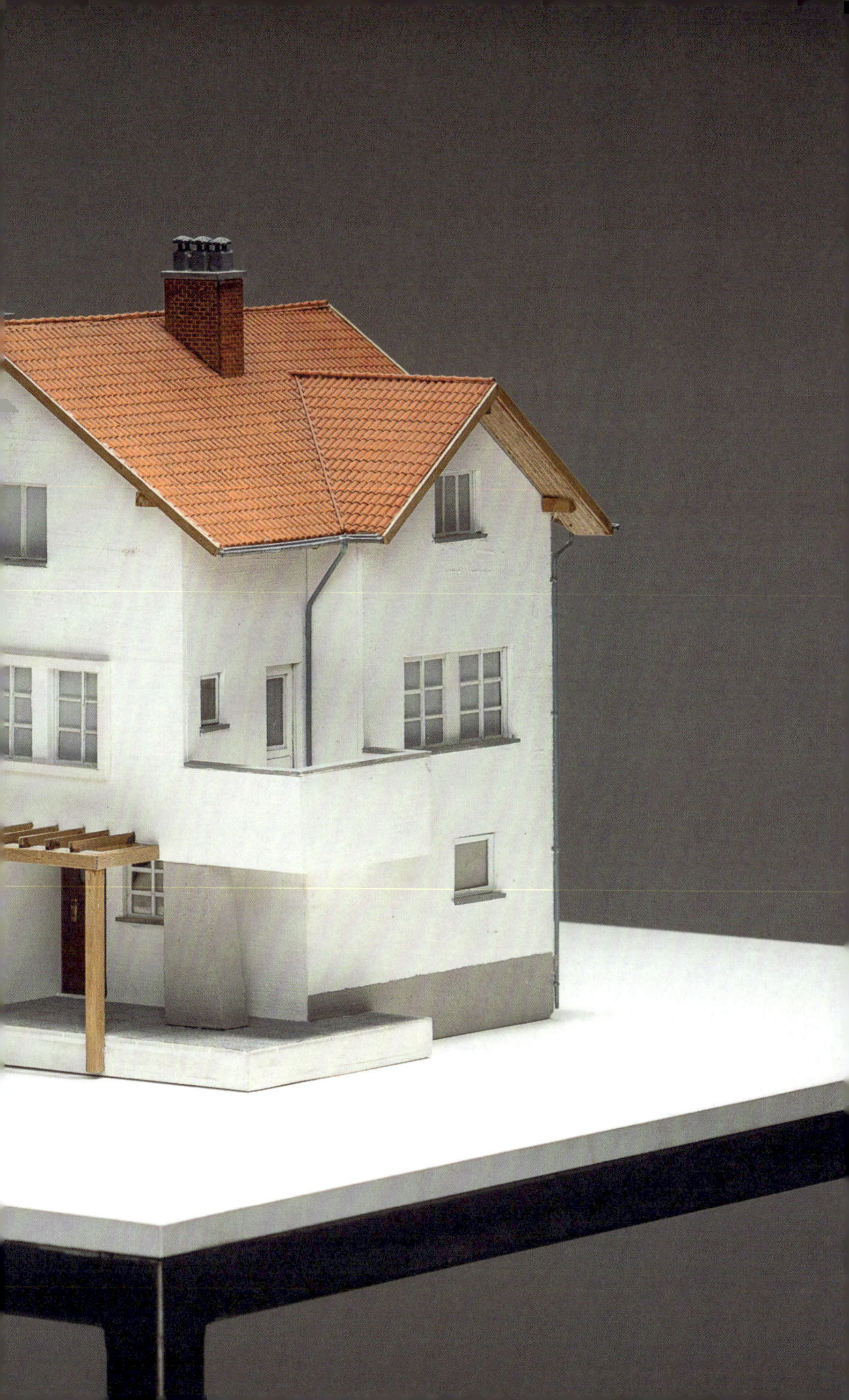

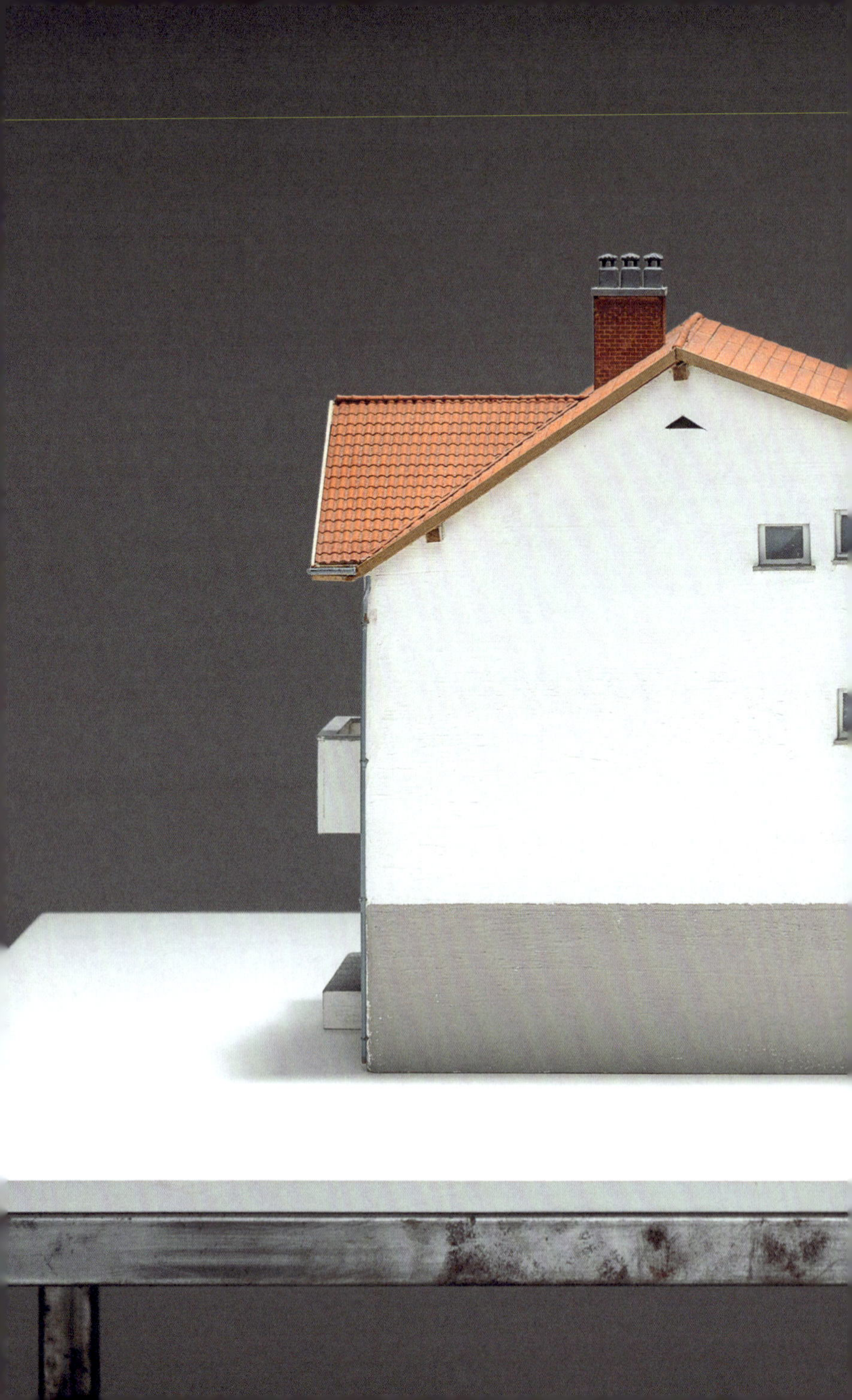

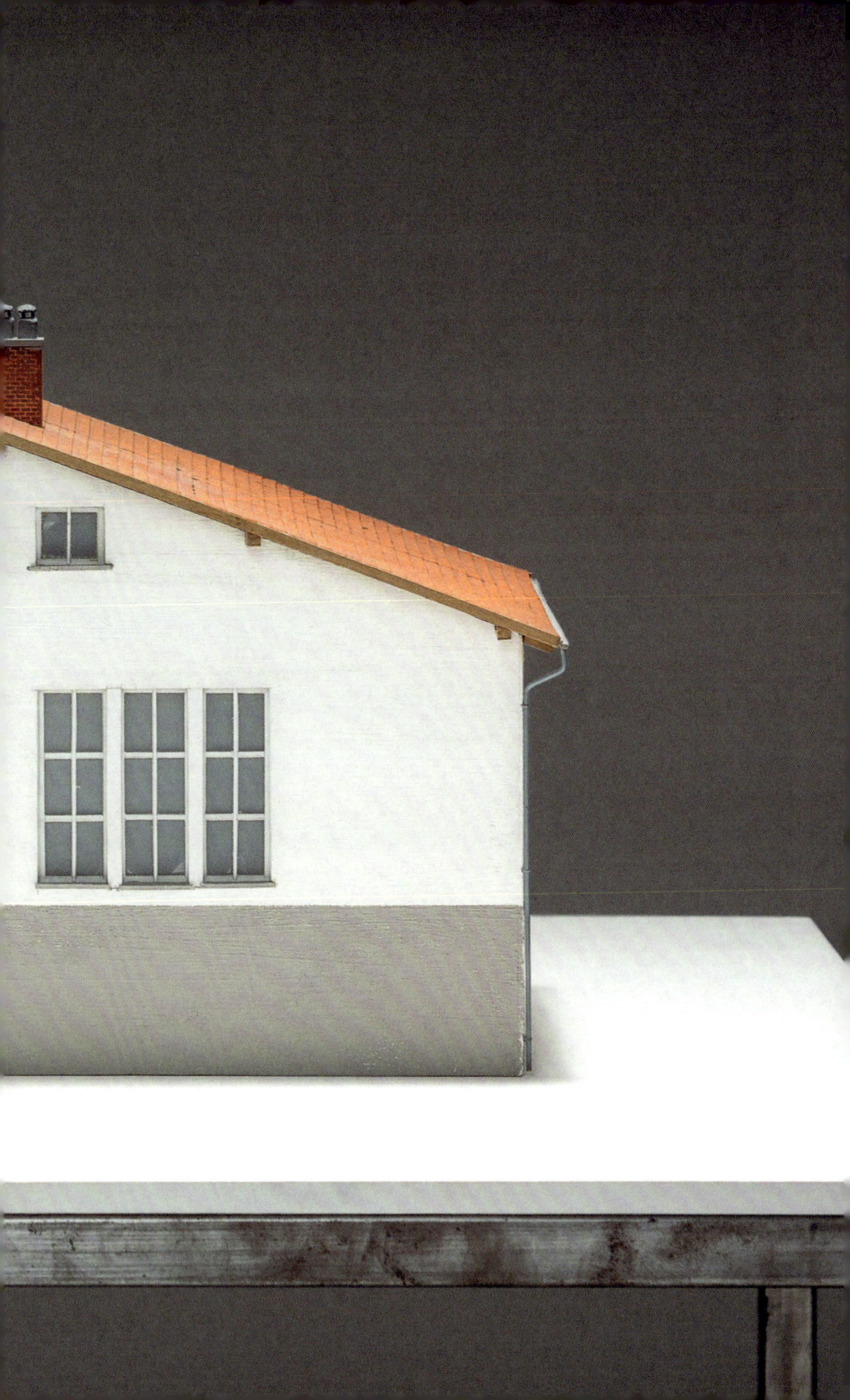

*Gründbergstraße 22, 2012*

# The Door Beneath the Pergola

## *Mark Z. Danielewski*

Any moment now the house will wake.

A hint of smoke drifts from the tallest chimney.
Soon more smoke finds a way up the second chimney.

Later curtains on the balcony window slide aside.
The glass stays black. Inside looks too dark to live.

But the house knows better. Inside matters least.

Rain falls. Water trips down the roof. The gutters fill as if
wild with laughter. Downspouts river the earth below already bright
with grass. Old roots and new growth conspire to vine the pergola.
The rain recedes but petals wild with whites and violet find the sun.

By moonlight more curtains ease apart.
Each pane greets each star passing through.

Where seven windows wait ivy befriends a wall satisfied long
before reaching an attic vent where a hummingbird builds her nest.

Morning fog glistens blade and leaf. Beneath the gable
a spider weaves a web and grants dawn a glimpse of night.

Starlings draw a cape around a breeze.
A song thrush flies into his reflection and dies.

The tree when it comes surprises the balcony too far to reach
with offers of stone fruit come late summer.

The snow surprises too tumbling off in slabs
before making peace with the roof's slant.

And then curtains return and opaque every frame. I was wrong.
The smoke that declared sleep's end no longer dares to play at clouds.
Doubt takes away every moment born to the house. What was
imminent leaves no room for explanation. As if here too waits
something too still for sleep and the imagination.

But the house knows better. What I thought matters least.

A bear ambles by the tree and rubs her great back against a corner
of the house then peers up at the balcony where a crow lands.
The ensuing rapture of caws and grunts lasts a long time.

When has a bear ever passed this way?
Will it happen again?

Two more crows land to hail the moment.

Icicles build the sky a crown.

The sky laughs. The sky has no need for a crown.
Nor does the house. Even a crown that's upside down.

The house knows better. What lasts forever matters least.

The pergola thickens green. Blooms spring raptures of smells
while bees announce young flowers and ants tidy up the bony mess
winter left behind. A cat missing an ear with some whiskers white
the rest black finds a step warm as noon and curls up. He completely
misses the fawn and doe. They gallop through the walls as if walls were
no more. Song thrushes too. Followed by rabbits. A dog.

In the storm that must answer lightning strikes a branch from
the cherry tree. Only the fallen branch burns. An owl on a sill
beneath the only gable without a nest watches as rain mutes fire
into embers into gray. By morning the owl is gone. A frog evades a snake.
A squirrel barks at a maple leaf. Two voles race from a burrow. A shadow
above darkens them all but passes on.

A goat and donkey come up to eat the grass as if no house could stand
there.

A window is open. Another window opens.

Any moment now the door beneath the pergola will open.

The house knows nothing. What happens next matters least.

*Pour Laure,*

# The View from Green Mountain

## *Céline Minard*

Just below the roof, the boy had set up his telescope. The tripod was locked in place, the window open over the garden. It was chilly out.

The night before, he had come across the teepee from when he was six, forever ago, he had set it up so the eyepiece would fit comfortably in the opening of the door that wasn't one, he had adjusted the viewing angle, the focal length, the focus, and he had gone to bed as if everything was normal. Everyone said good-night to him without any inkling.

Extraordinary experiences are a matter of patience and preparation.

Back at his post beneath the roof, swathed in his quilt, he was waiting for the lights, the real ones, to come out. He had counted his envelopes: his pajamas, the sleeping bag, the teepee, the house. He could have used a hat but he didn't want to arouse any suspicions, he didn't move. Ramrod-straight, cozy and cross-legged within the down, angled toward the rectangle of the open window, he inhaled the damp air as if it carried subtle details that might confirm his hypotheses.

Ever since last summer, the moon's face had changed considerably.

He had long since outgrown fairy tales. The lies that

Lucian had told and the rants that Tobias, convinced he was that much smarter for being held back a year, had unleashed had all made him smile. In his eyes, Méliès's cinematographic inventions were child's play. But if the moon wasn't a face, whether calm or contorted, nor any sort of mirror, or ocean, then it couldn't be a desert of gray lava.

The boy had clear ideas.

There was silica, magnesia, and quicklime, yes. But there was water and it was frozen.

There was the unsmiling face that was visible, and then there was the other face. The one full of holes. It could be seen by those under six and the boy knew that his launch window, his final one, was now opening up in front of him.

He knew how to travel on a ray of light, how to go through the eyepiece, how to get back, he was ready.

Getting past the atmosphere was nothing, not even a hiccup, he waved to the geostationary satellites, and then straight ahead into the oil slick without a ripple or breeze, a blackness that had no up or down, an asteroid here and there, an old probe welcoming him, and then the Sea of Crises in a fell swoop and he landed, ankle-deep in the powder snow, pulling back deliberately, and cupped his hands around his mouth and his warm breath as he took in the landscape.

A magnificent bleakness.

He saw the footprints of the two men who had touched down last summer—Earth time—some residue just south-southeast. His eyes rested on it and passed on. The maps were a joke; things would get more complicated now.

Because he knew the Nagel's Encyclopedia Guide inside and out, he hadn't brought it. A handful of raisins and a few meters of butcher's twine were his only indulgences.

He headed west to the Lakos cliffs and crossed them

with carefully calculated jumps. An easy enough path, just eight flat stretches, the last one barely bigger than a cinder block but oriented such that a gentle push of his right toe got him clear to the top. The Sea of Tranquility stretched out beneath his feet, its swaying barely perceptible. He put two hefty stones in his pockets and jumped, instinctively holding his breath. He slid halfway down, angled his body rightward to avoid Cape Kangaroo, and kept going toward the mouth of the Sea of Nectar. The regolith came up to his knees, billowed up then drifted away in his wake. The channel between the two seas was narrow, and he steered clear of the Theophilus Crater, barely avoided its counterpart, and went straight into Nectar. The terrain there was sloshing, he had to be careful not to stay put, the pull was slow yet inexorable and his socks were already starting to get soaked. Once he'd found his rhythm, it felt like being on a hoverboard, not flat on the ground but not floating either, he worked his way through the dense surface. His regular movement, carefully calibrated even on the down, was soothing, bordering on hypnotic. The sight of Mons Huygens brought him back to his senses. He took the stones out of his pockets. As the twentieth parallel approached he saw the outskirts of the massive area that was the Field of Drops, turned toward Tycho, and took a great leap over the silvery-gray plateau; its mantle, being far springier than Nectar's, launched him over three small craters with a single bound. The boy steadied himself at the edge of a scalloped depression, sighed, and focused properly.

He would have enjoyed looking at Mons Leibnitz which he knew a bit, but there wasn't enough time. The clearest route to the south pole was, without a question, the knottiest one, through the Field of Drops. He'd stop at Marinus and

Clavius before the long descent that was the reason he was standing here, at the top of an unnamed crater with a rim as gentle as a beagle's ears.

He decided to eat his first raisin here. 384,402 kilometers from his house. He felt proud at how far he'd come yet keenly aware of how far he still had to go. He didn't reminisce about the warm quilt abandoned in his teepee, beneath his telescope's eyepiece. The Urfahraner Markt fair was where he'd figured it all out. The shooting gallery was rigged. He'd watched the air-gun pellet push into the balloon's surface, almost to the breaking point, and then bounce back, springing off the insidiously reinforced plastic. The moon isn't a frozen bit of Earth. It was entirely to be expected that the moon and the earth had collided. The boy had clear ideas and he'd come there to confirm them.

His journey to the south pole was cumbersome but unwavering. The Drops didn't scare him, he dealt with them one by one, determinedly, indefatigably. Each depression had a small hill at its center, and if he went down fast and light enough, he'd end up on the little mountain's summit without too much work, perfectly positioned for the next slope. He simply had to bend his knees just so, hug the curves to hit the peaks, teeter on the slope and smile, and most of all set and maintain the pace.

Resting in the fine powder of Clarius, he ate two more raisins.

Ten craters further south, he felt the ground plunge sharply downward. He'd just crossed the perceptible horizon. His telescope in the teepee had just lost sight of him, he knew. The dimensions were out of proportion. The entire pole seemed to sink toward a single indefinite point that he could tell was immense. And then he was on the edge.

The moon's crust yawned beneath his feet, a dizzyingly vast, deeply blue fissure. A blinding blue that beggared his imagination. He got down on his belly, shut his eyes, and counted his envelopes—the pajamas, the quilt, the teepee, the house (one was missing)—until his breathing was normal again. Then he looked, and saw where to go. The center, down there, where a drab, near-white reflection gleamed deep within the shimmering color.

He had to weigh himself down. He drew out the four meters of butcher's twine and started tying huge rocks nearby to his waist. He didn't stand back up, there was no need, he was the wrong way around. He had to crawl forward quickly along the rock face to get back down. If he stopped, even with the ballast, he'd go back up, or, worse, he'd be stuck in the astronomical passage indefinitely, with no wind or wave to push him or carry him. He didn't waver, he dove in. The only breeze was from his movement. He went all out, grabbed every rough surface, pulled with his fingers, pushed with his toes. The jutting basalt and anorthosite bits were at once springboards and a breath of air. He shot like a rocket in reverse toward the fault's center. Suddenly—curled up, smaller than a woodlouse, lighter than a balloon—his energy scared him and he stopped on an outcrop. There, on the ceiling without any effort, supine yet upside-down, he saw the pulpy mass of metal pulling him like a magnet. He touched its surface after one last nose-dive, flabbergasted and shaking. The mass was warm, soft, molten—he had taken off his gloves. It seemed to tremble within the emptiness and hardened lava framing it, a multipotent unearthly energy that wasn't the past. That was never the past.

His hypothesis was confirmed, and tomorrow he would be ten years old. It was finished now. A hunter-god, a gambler-god, maybe goddess, a giantess had indeed shot in the gallery of the solar system's orbs. Only the moon had retained this pellet.

The way the world, the moon, their course, Kepler's dream and the quilt's softness all interlocked was crystal-clear.

He could go back up. Hold his breath and push off with his heel, jump straight up from the pole over the horizon. His telescope, locked in place on his tripod on the third floor beneath the roof of Gründbergstrasse 22 in Linz, would see him and bring him back along the ray of light in the blink of an eye. A clear-sighted one.

Hardly enough to call him a wizard.

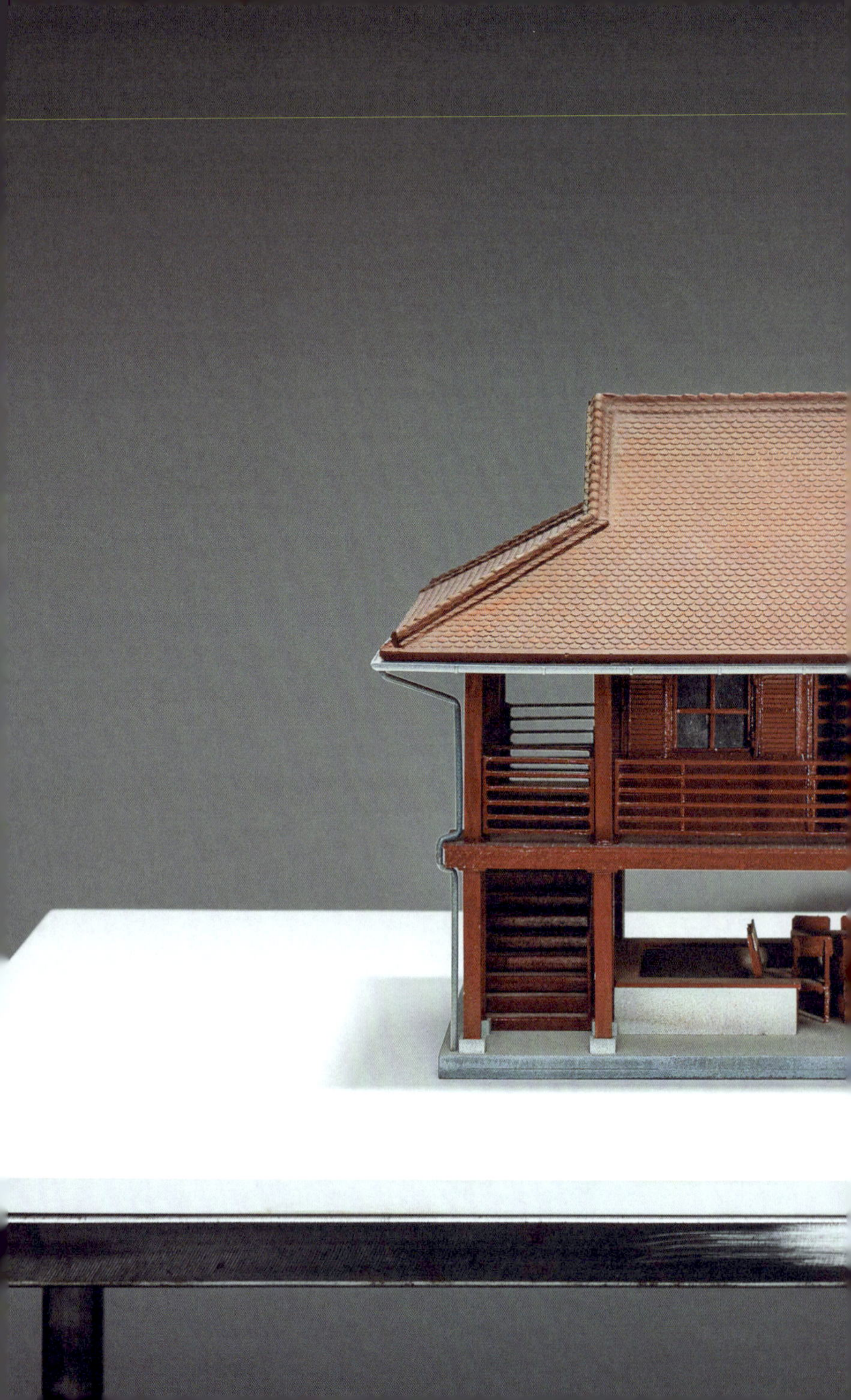

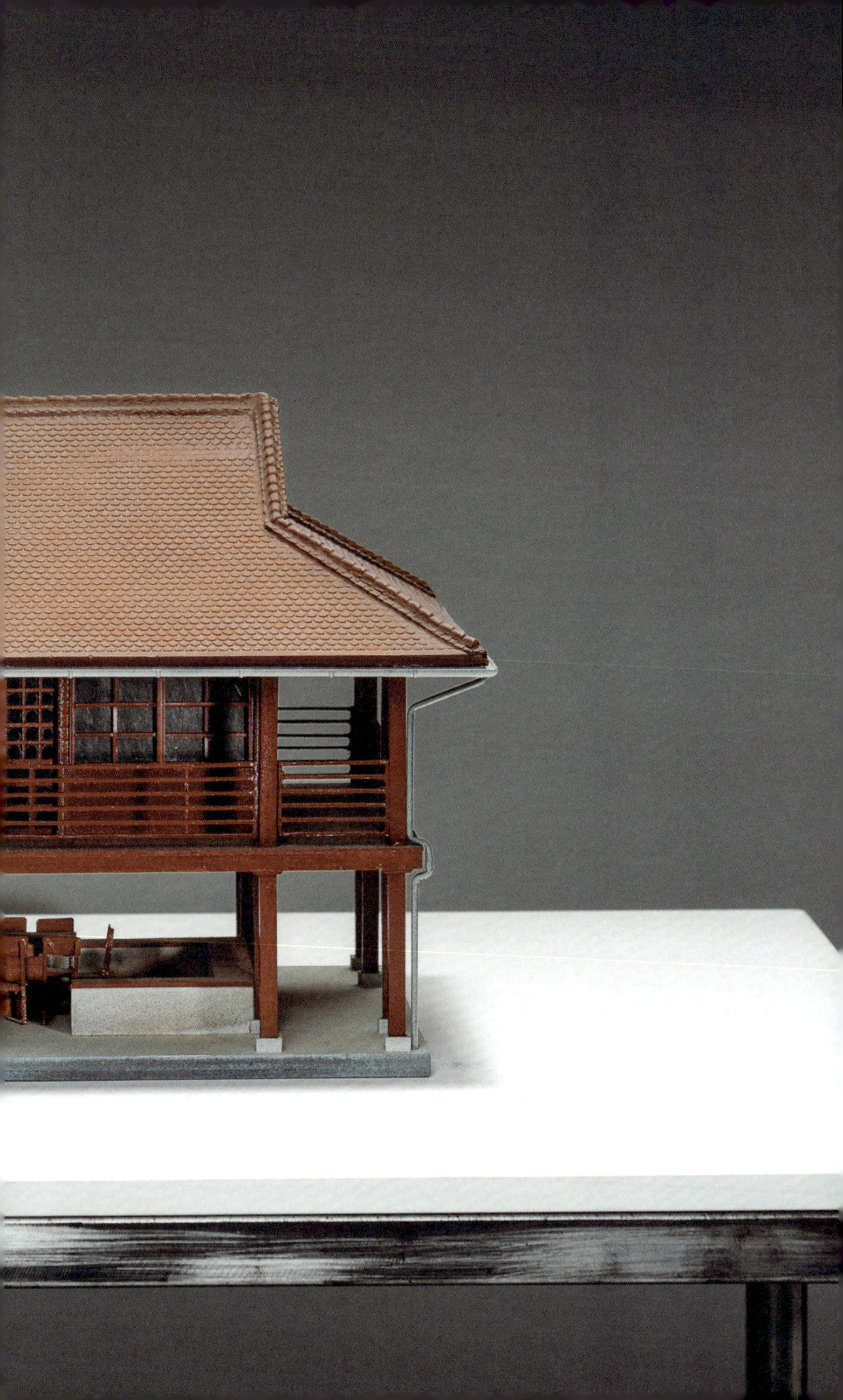

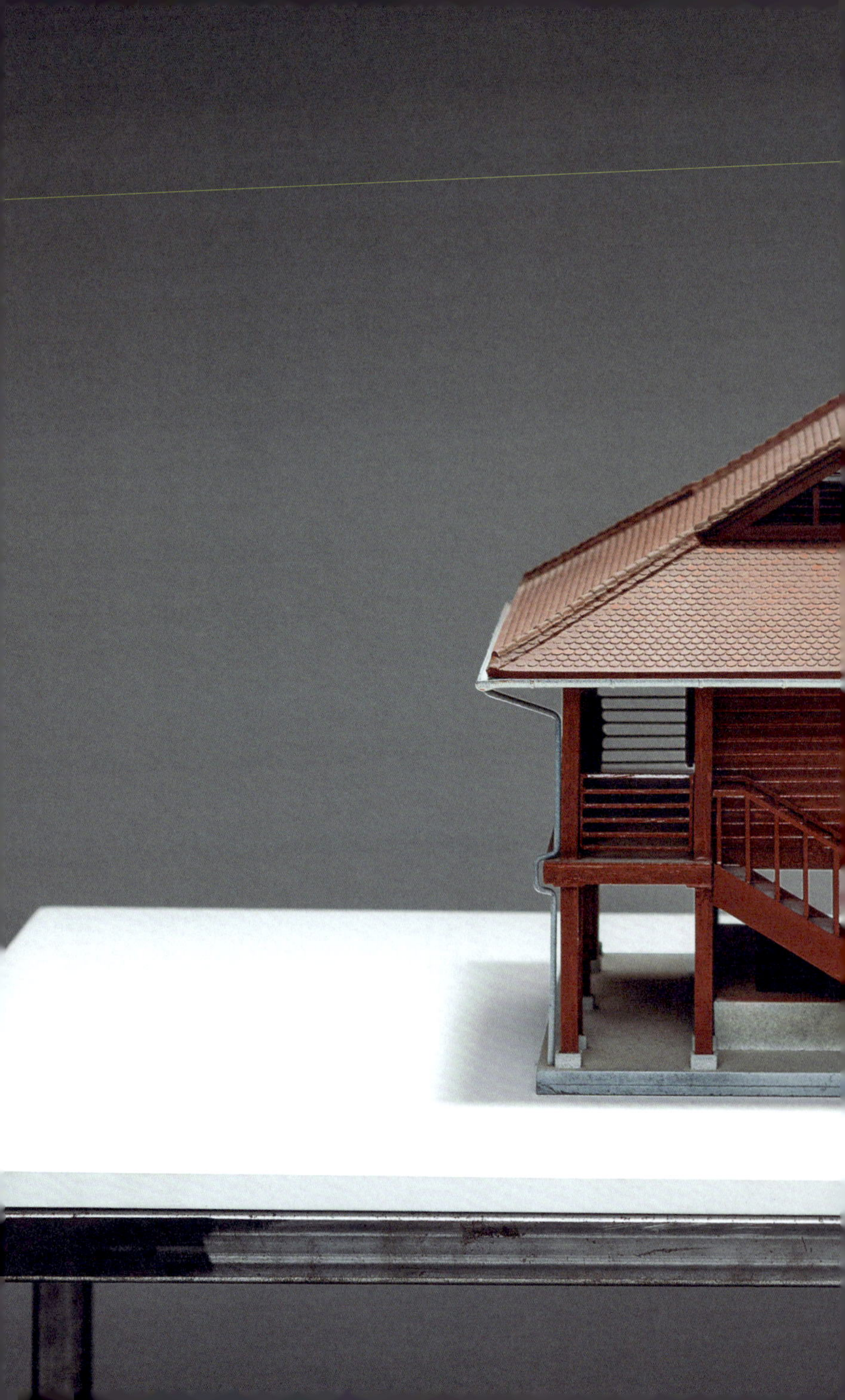

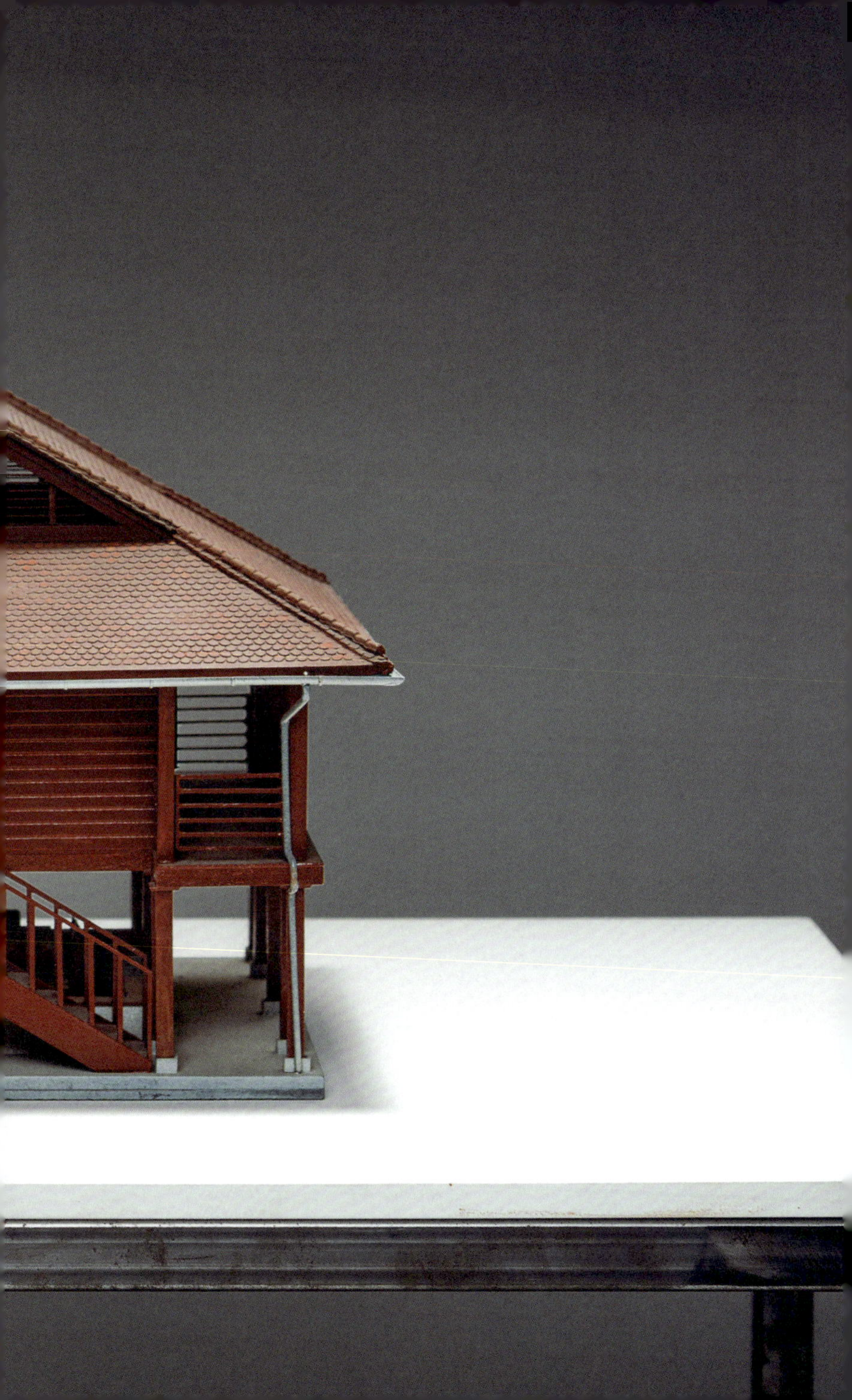

*Uncle Ho,* 2012

# Some Architectural Considerations

## *Ann Cotten*

How do we build a state?
The longer the house is
the longer must be the porch.

What to place at the core?
There will be violence,
answered with violence,
there will be sly violence,
coming ahead of preemted sly violence.
Hot heads are needed
what shall cool them?

What to place at the core?
While the forces arise
and need the structures
they fear the structures
formed by
the carrying madness
carrying the madness

formed by
days of splashing through
fields of ancestors
in neverending ending.

From all they know
and that they know
this is the end
of all they know
and all they don't know.

It is the beginning,
but the beginning is too big.
We need a house.

We need a house
built in a way
that lets us think
out of the space
that we have learned to think in
without thinking about
the space we learned
to think in, or not too much.

It is a house in which
one talks to one's parents
when one has become adult,
as adult and adult,
later as adult and a child.
It is a house where children
run around naked in the same place
one ran and slid oneself and one slides

past them on one's knees
and see ones parents afresh,
it is a house
in which anger passes
ideas settle and dry
for use next season,
but can be husked and used sooner
if needed.

And the small breasts
at the top of the stair
like morning and evening star,
tease young and old
tease women and men
tell children
the sky twinkles like the earth
as they climb the stair

with their space between.

This house is order
and space, for the air
to waft through
carrying new wind,
new rain.

* * *

How can they think?
They need to be cooled.
Wind must blow through
between Paris and China.

Promises and their slow
cracking into shards.
Wind must come through.

How to let us think?
In the gap between lips
between words
let there be seen
a steady place to be
where the wind blows
touches us
without saying anything.

⋆ ⋆ ⋆

How do we build a state?
It is with the space between.
From house to house
a days walk.
From arm to arm
the weight of two pails.
A pillar, measuring respect,
carries the roof.

They will not join if we say
too much. They know that
there may be things that
we have had to say
to make a space
for things to happen.

They do not speak except for
the fact that they help us in every way
and do whatever is needed.

How do we build a state?
The longer the house is
the longer must be the porch.

How do we build a state?
So that everyone will help
it must be recognizable
we cannot build it on words
nor on the hot blood
it is the space where you want to be
when the wind blows.

How do you make your day?
It is as long as my eye is clear
or someone else's eye is clear
after that I fall
and it will go on without me.

Your face
is the sun that rises every day
more wrinkled, and is walking about
with hands swinging, falling like rain
on the rice that rises to meet
your face, and it will never
be tired, it will never
be tired.

How do we build a state?
We do not dig into the ground.
We do not explain to the satellites.
If you are with us you are here.
There has been longing fueling these
secret words
but between them and the world
in which we could live
and face the old longing
now long gone
with faces wrinkled and tired,—

Ohimé—

there is a space.

How do we build a state?

The longer the house is
the longer must be the porch.

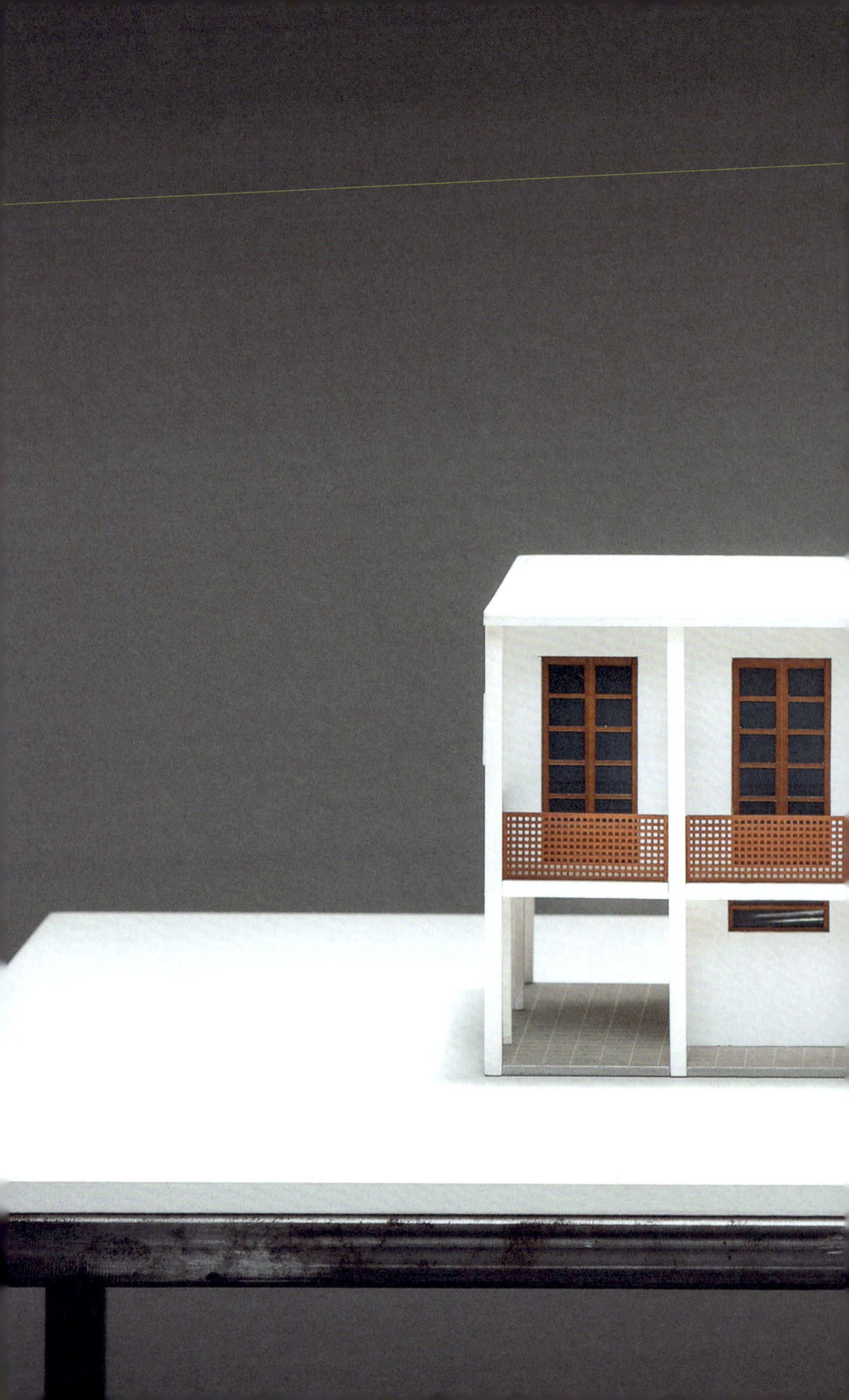

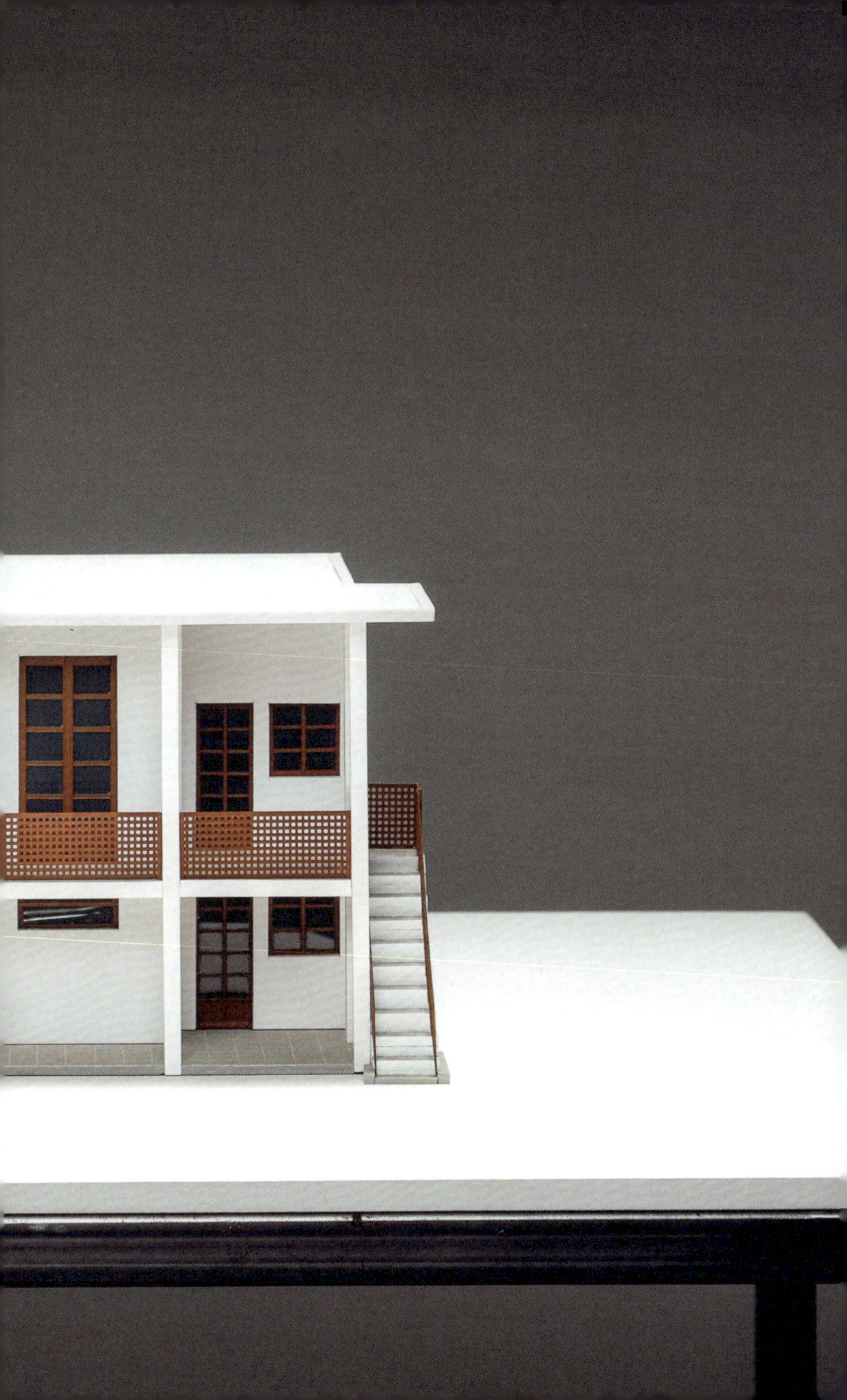

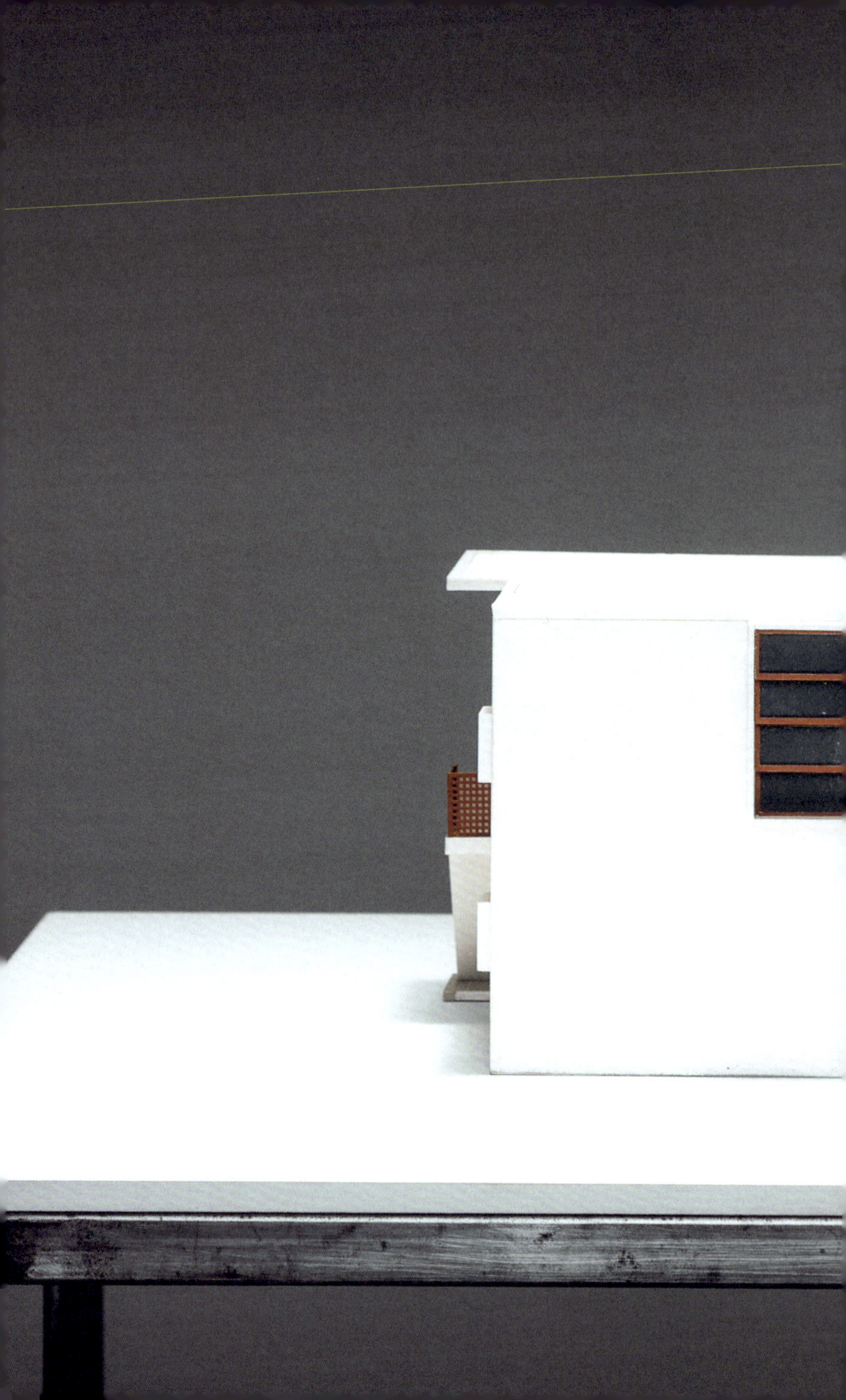

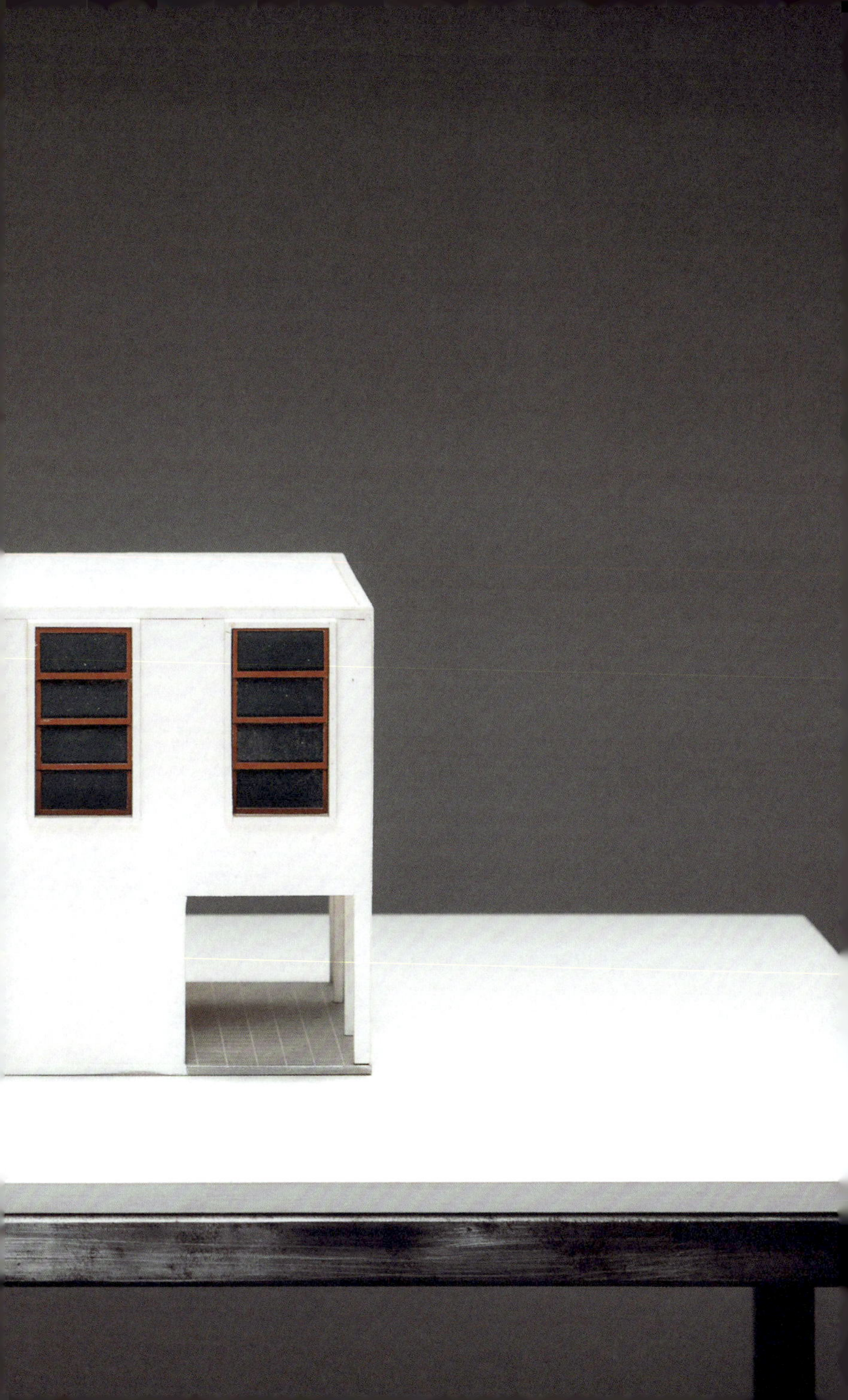

## *Villa tropicale*, 2012–13

# Villa tropicale
## *Karen Pinkus*

Imagine this villa as a model for a stage set. What kind of drama might be imagined to take place here? The characters: A family of Italian colonizers, settling in "for the rest of their lives" taking refuge from the torrid climate and relentless African dust outside (these are the words of Luigi Piccinato, the architect).* A few native servants. An Italian wet nurse and nanny, of course—can't have the babies exposed to inferior milk or grow too attached.

Our colonizing family is supposed to thrive (but then, Italy never got far enough to establish themselves in Africa, hence the permanent dwelling as a fantasy). Perhaps the most banal sort of Oedipal plot is played out here, echoing Italy's attempt to reclaim its glorious paternal past in "its" Mediterranean, but finding itself undercut by those feminized other democracies or abject feminized colonial subjects. Maybe in the final scene the father takes the upper hand, though, establishing order.

Or ours might be a surrealist architectural spectacle,

* Technically speaking, Libya, the place of Italian colonialism, is not part of the tropics, although Italian East Africa (AOI) is. Piccinato wrote an essay on the ideals of colonial houses for *Domus* (19:6, 1936).

like a metaphysical painting (think de Chirico) come to life, with statues uttering different signifiers Italians used in their attempts to establish an "official" Fascist style of building (in Italy as well as the colonies): Functionalist! Rational! Modern! Mediterranean! For contrast, locals might shout out terms like Moorish, Decorative, Baroque, Eclectic or International. The scene could shift to tents or tukuls—thatched huts—of natives, displaced by the Italians from dense urban areas to decrease their power, abject in their nomadism compared with the permanence of the villa.

We might see foldable temporary shelters—products of Italian ingenuity—that could be assembled or disassembled in a day. We might see Italian tourists, making the Fascist salute as they get ready to board cruise ships for home.

Then, back to the villa. Perhaps through the thick white walls we hear the cry of an Italian newborn. Perfectly healthy, robust, uncontaminated by the outside.

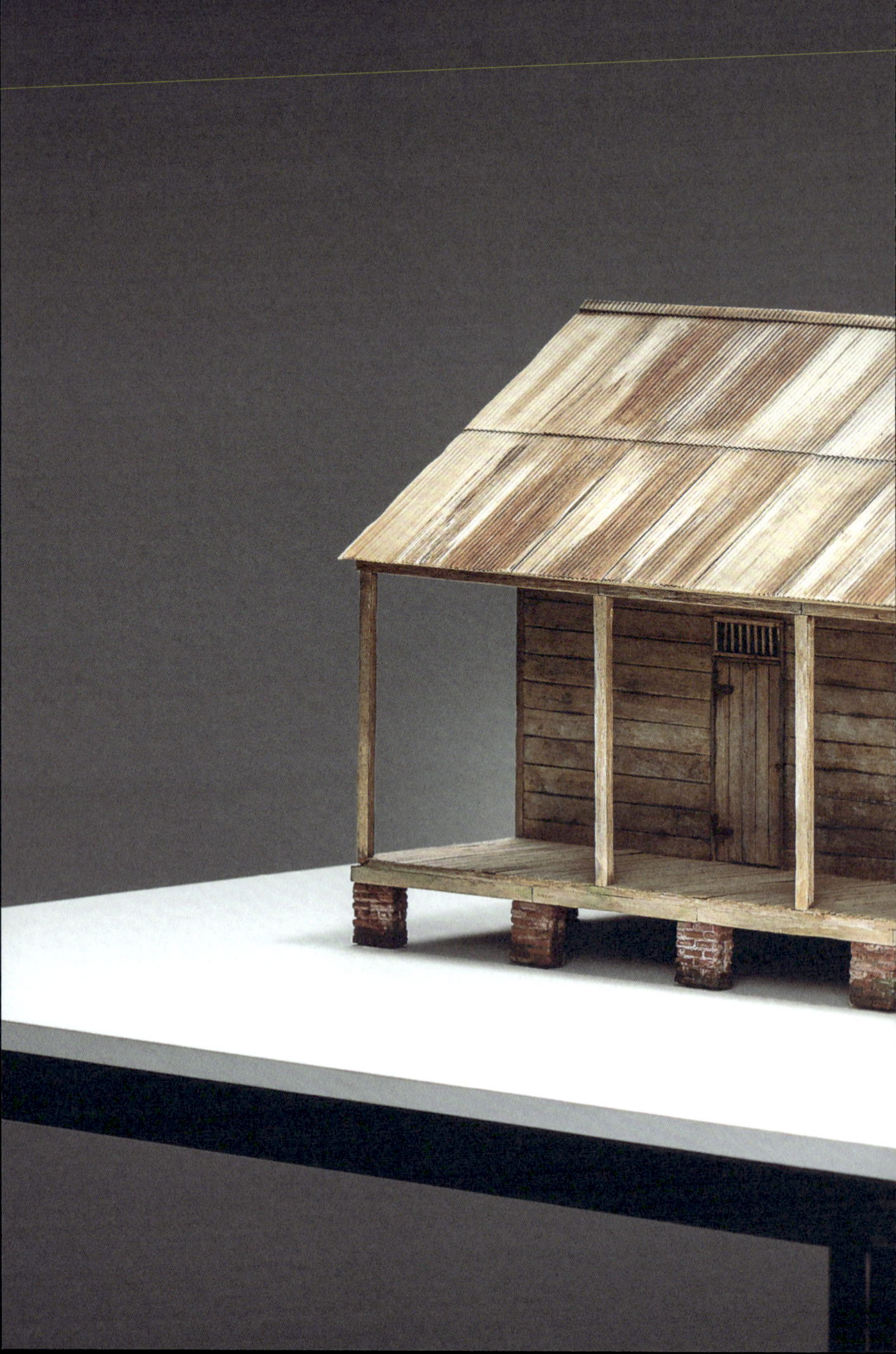

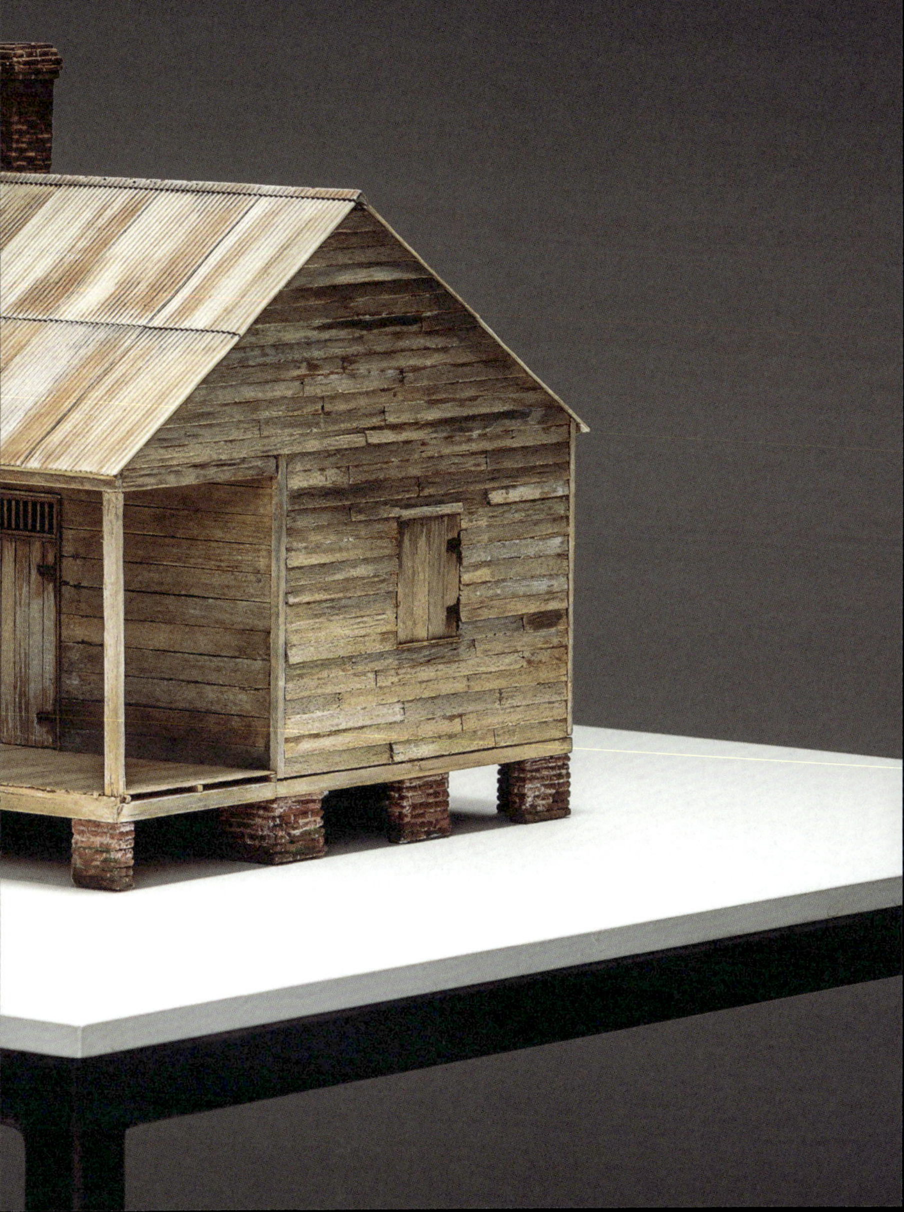

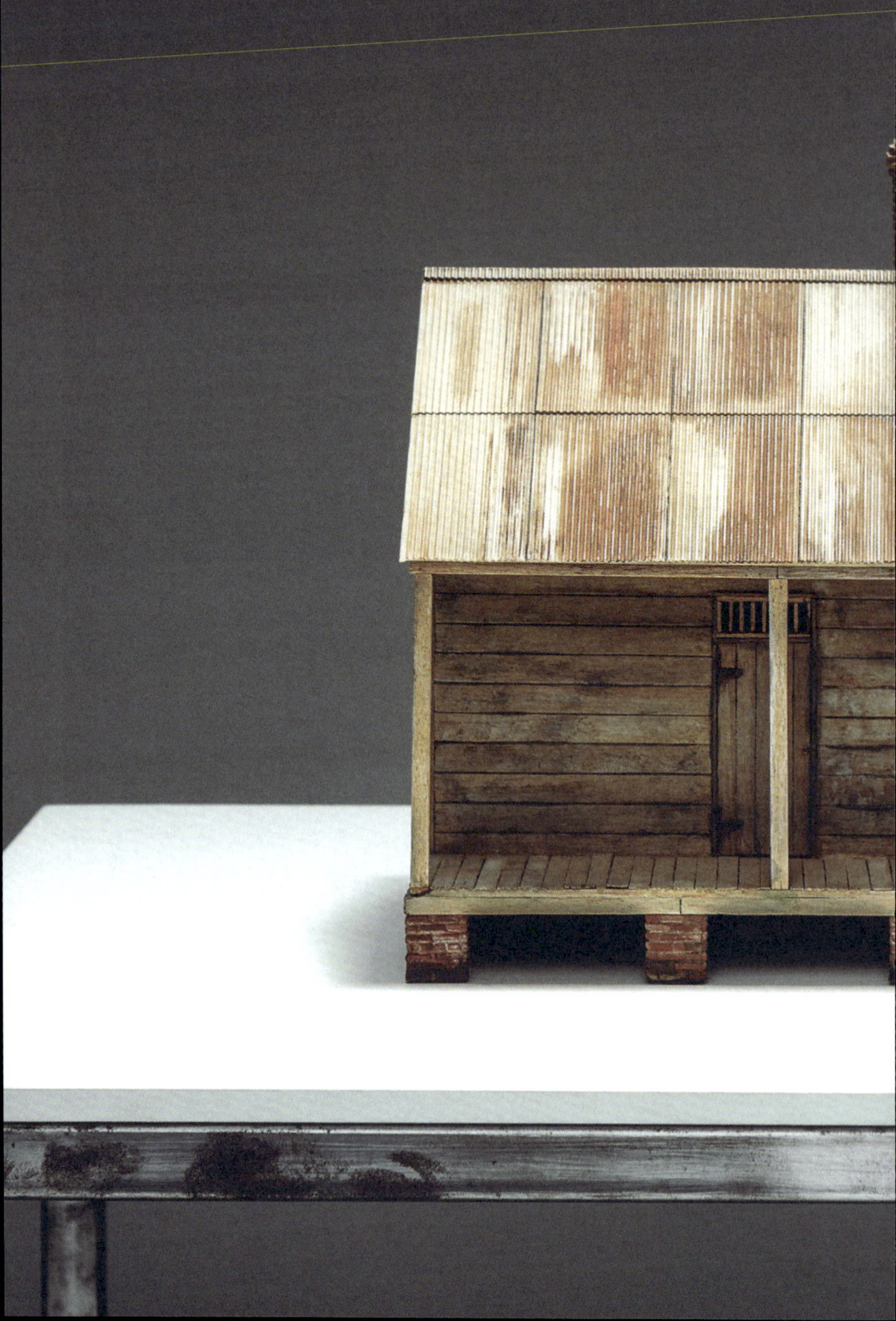

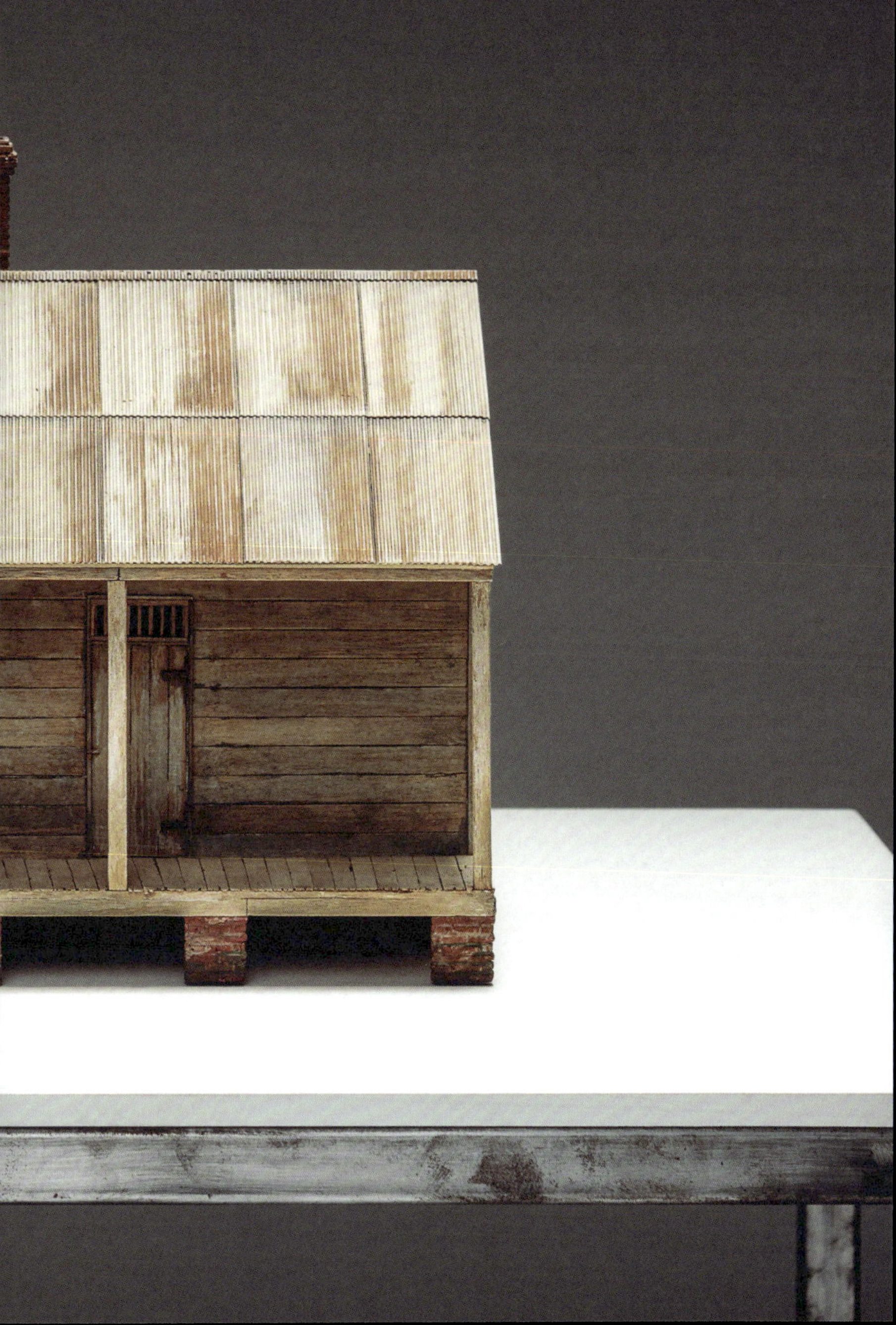

*Evergreen*, 2013

*Dionne Brand*

# Evergreen and

Laura, Monticello, Montpelier Camden, Sabine Hall,
Boldrup, Flowerdew, Boone Hall, White Hall, Hampton,
Woodland, Hermatage, Gainswood, Laurel Valley, (NA)
Good Hope, Potosi, Roaring River, Adelphi, Aeolus
Valley, Aqualta Vale, Air Mount and Newmarket, Aleppo,
Amity Hall, San Ambrosio, El Reposo, Anse Mahuat,
Brechin Castle Estate, (C) Berbice, Corentyne, Aurora,
Bathsheba's Lust, Belle Plain, Better Success, Blenhein,
Brothers, Canefield, Berbice, Cornelia Ida, Demerarra,
De Kinderen and Boode's Rust, Deutichem, De Liesde,
Doornhaag, De Eendragt and Mon Repos, Nomen
Nescio and Enfield, Garden of Eden, Demerarra.
Santa Eufrasia, Vale do Paraiba, Reconcavo, Cachoeira,
Abrantes, Agua de Meninos, (SA) …

It is endless … endless … Ever green. Interminable architecture, side gables, single piles, wall, insubstantial, ancillary piers, brick, dirt, wood, clay and stick, kettle, iron, boiling, wattle and daub, bake oven, dentil, lattice, pilaster, rectangular days … and minutes like a grizzled beam …

24.71 million $km^2$ plus 17.84 million $km^2$ plus 521,876 $km^2$ plus 324,000 $km^2$

NA plus SA plus CA plus C equals something, something, some thing incalculable.

And what we made of these inconsiderable kilometres:
Breathing.

The way we dissolved into doorways: Salvage

What we calculated: Ribbons

What we lifted open: Eyes

May 2, 1766. Jack ▇▇▇ promoting the late disorderly meetings, ▇▇▇ is gone off ▇▇▇

Oct. 10, 1767. JUPITER ▇▇▇ stirring up ▇▇▇ an insurrection, ▇ a great Newlight preacher. ROBIN ▇▇▇ 25 ▇▇▇ brother to Jupiter. DINAH ▇▇▇ near 6 feet high ▇▇▇ mother ▇▇▇ carried with them ▇ , an old blue duffle great coat, one bearskin, a scarlet jacket, and a fine new linen shirt. ▇▇▇ They will endeavor ▇▇▇ southward.

Oct. 20, 1768 ▇▇▇ Jude ▇▇▇ remarkable ▇▇▇ running away since she was ten years old ▇▇▇ a free woman ▇▇▇

She went away in her winter clothing.

May 11, 1769. PETER, 44 a white Virginia cloth waistcoat and petticoat, a Tarlton plaid gown, and sundry other of his wife's clothes; a gun of an uncommon large size, and a fiddle.

September 1, 1772. Girl named *Thursday* Had on a red Cloth Petticoat, a red Baize Bed Gown, and red Ribbon about her Head. Trouble.

June 16, 1775 SAM carried several things with him an old bay horse, an iron pot, a narrow axe, a handsaw, and an old smooth bore gun.

Santa Eufrasia, Vale do Paraiba, Reconcavo, Cachoeira, Abrantes, Agua de Meninos, (SA) Good Hope, Potosi, Roaring River, Adelphi, Aeolus Valley, Aqualta Vale, Air Mount and Newmarket, Aleppo, Amity Hall, San Ambrosio, El Reposo, Anse Mahuat, Brechin Castle Estate, (C) Berbice, Corentyne, Aurora, Bathsheba's Lust, Belle Plain, Better Success, Blenhein, Brothers, Canefield, Berbice, Cornelia Ida, Demerarra, De Kinderen and Boode's Rust, Deutichem, De Liesde, Doornhaag, De Eendragt and Mon Repos, Nomen Nescio and Enfield, Garden of Eden, Demerarra, (SA) Laura, Montecello, Montpelier Camden, Sabine Hall, Boldrup, Flowerdew, Boone Hall, White Hall, Hampton, Woodland, Hermatage, Gainswood, Laurel Valley … (NA)

Is … unbroken … Ever green. Unrelieved architecture, side gables, single piles, hall, insubstantial, ancillary, piers, brick, extreme dirt, earth fast wood, clay and stick, kettle, unrelieved iron, systems architecture … one door and posts

24.71 million $km^2$ with the addition of 17.84 million $km^2$ and the dividend of 521,876 $km^2$ and the advantage of 324,000 $km^2$

Preposition, adjective, noun and conjunction, evergreen language, plus, piu, plus, et, all parts of speech, *summa de arithmetica:* NA ampersand SA mehr CA plus C equals infinity. Particularis de computis et scripturis, each day …

And what we made of these inconsiderable kilometres:
Interiors.

The way we dissolved into doorways: Provinces

What we calculated: Ellipses

What we lifted open: The Lids of Mornings

# Evergreen

## *Hanif Abdurraqib*

With Julian in Oxford, we survey the green leaves leaping
from the edges of oak branches bending above the pristine
roof of the blue plantation house & the people outside
are pointing & marveling at its architecture & this, I think,
is how the hands vanish from the land & Julian says why
don't they ever take the people to the slave shacks & I imagine
the answer has to do with who does & doesn't see the blood
laid upon the fields where husbands & brides swear an oath
to love each other until one of them is buried under the land
& that land may, I think, also have a history & behind the blue
sprawl of the plantation house & somewhere beyond
the evergreen trees I can see the wood shack & its narrow
doors & I think about the bodies always & how many spilled
on top of other ones & I tell Julian they ain't got no shit like this
where I come from & what I mean is that I come from a place with a river
that slaves drowned in when trying to make it north & on the plaque
which sits at the opening mouth of the river there are no names & the river
is brown & when I was a boy, a man in my hood would say that at night
you could hear the voices of the drowned slaves rising & in Oxford,
Julian says even when we gone we ain't never really gone & I suppose this is true
& I suppose it is up to the wind to hold the stories & the names & the names
& the names & I suppose it is up to the water to tint itself brown & remind
an elder of death & who did not survive & they say the labor is unspeakable
but the money isn't & the question curling itself from the depths
of a darkened river & from the hooded green of trees is a simple one:

who will one day be a tour guide through the interior of your most painful history?

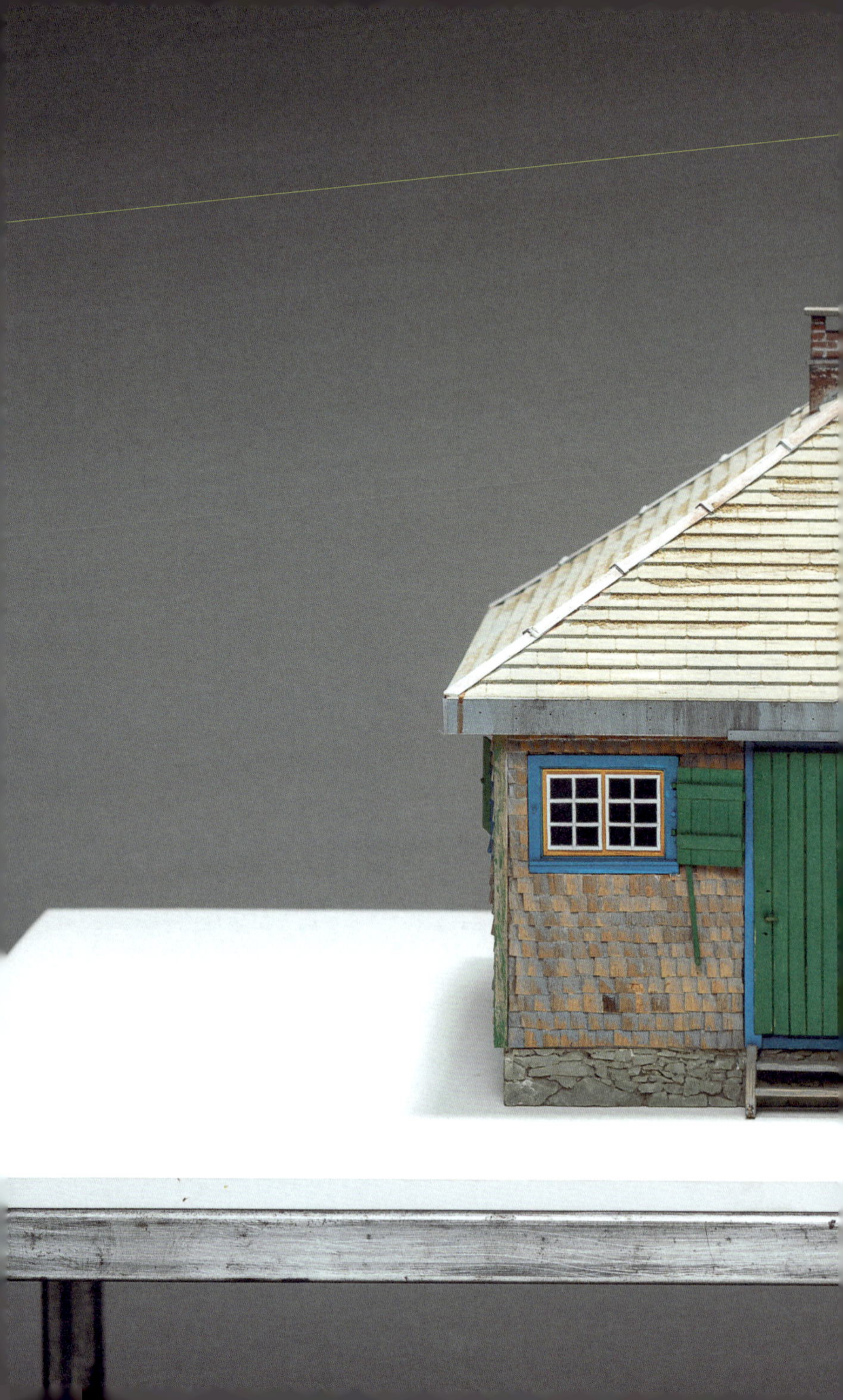

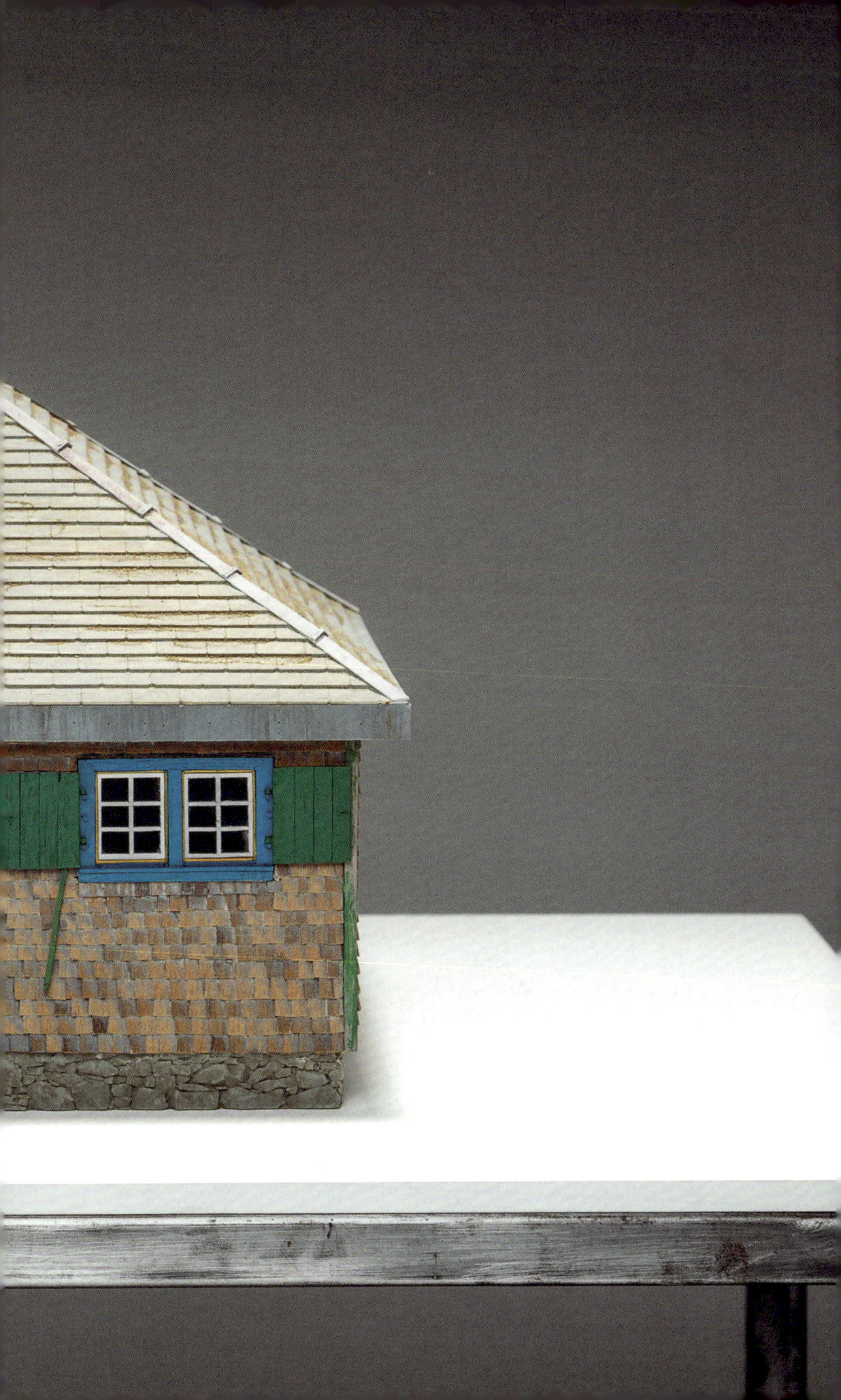

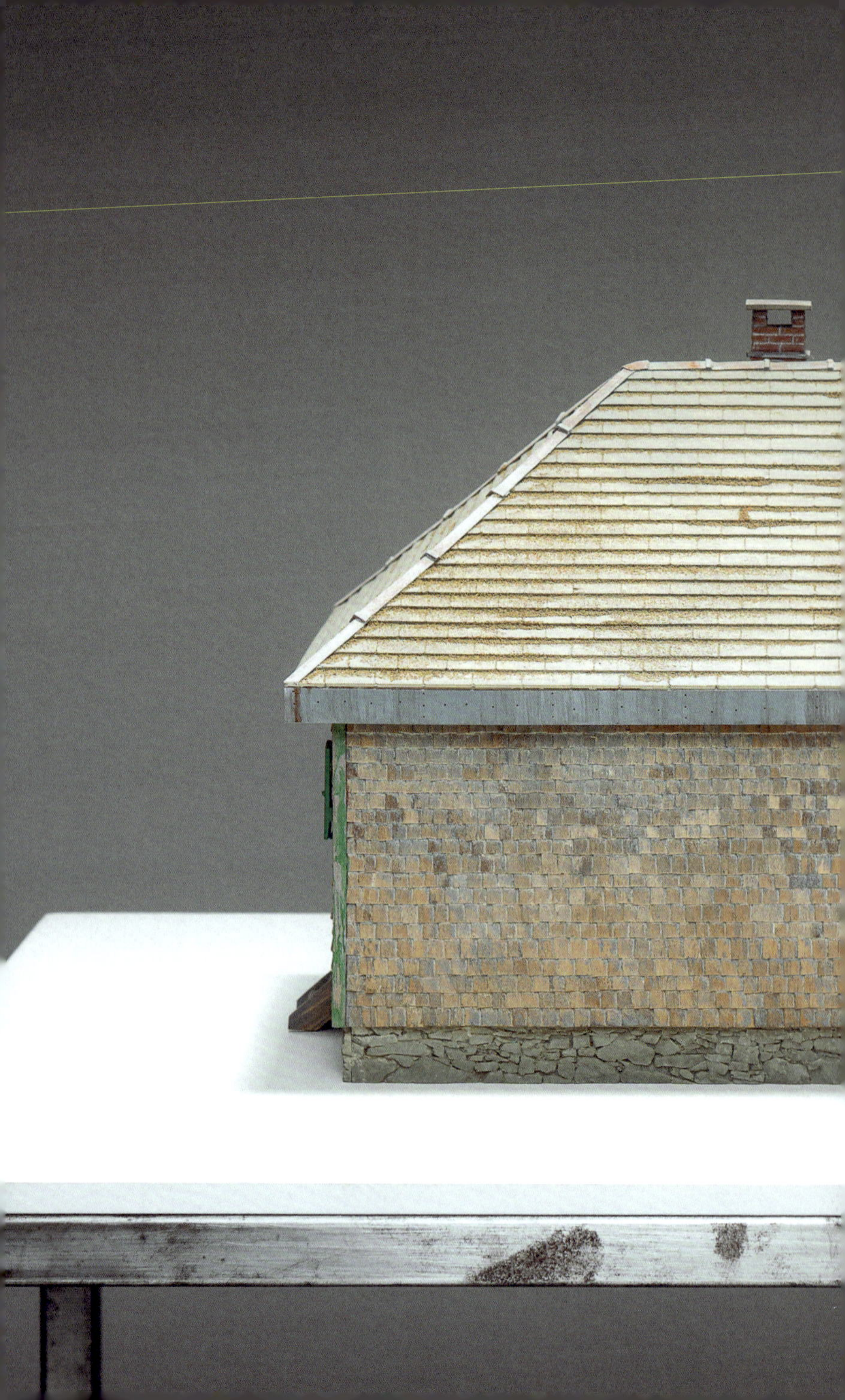

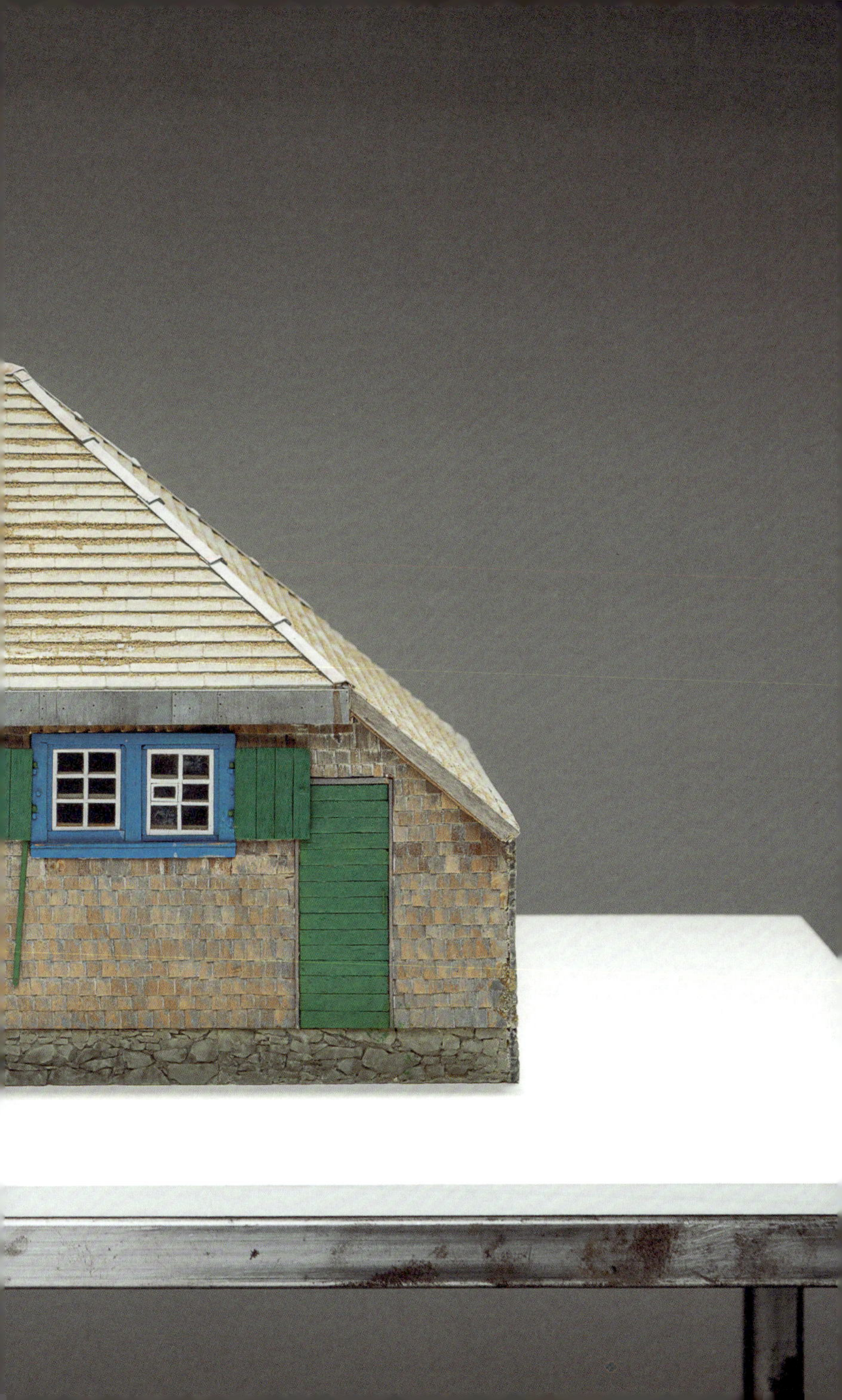

*Heidegger*, 2014

# Portrait of the Artist as a Little Heidegger

## *Davide Longo*

As for me, being about to build a house, I am only prepared to grieve for those who will die in it. My mother of course, but Tonio too, and the neighbor who calls me Professor; I shall suffer for them. Because they will be inside the house. But my cousins, even though they shared my early childhood, will be outside. When any of them dies, I'll just say "oh dear" and go back to my omelet. It'll be the same for those whose deaths reach me through the news, dying in earthquakes or in another country, or people who have never had any real future ahead of them. This is because there was a time when I used to suffer severely, without rhyme or reason, whenever I read of tragedies in the newspaper: one morning I might grieve for child soldiers in Africa, and the same evening feel nothing whatsoever for a friend knocked down by a bus. Someone whose death had deprived me of some of the best years of my life.

It used to be so much simpler: you would grieve for your wife or for a friend killed in battle, and feel virtually nothing for anything else. Now it's entirely different ... there's no point in dipping your finger in ointment and imagining you'll be able to massage your body all over. You must make a choice. So now I choose a small area and smear the unguent there. When I'm old my body will be more wizened than yours, but those few centimeters will still preserve the skin of the child I used to be. Because only the most deeply felt grief will have any meaning at all, as I've explained to you here.

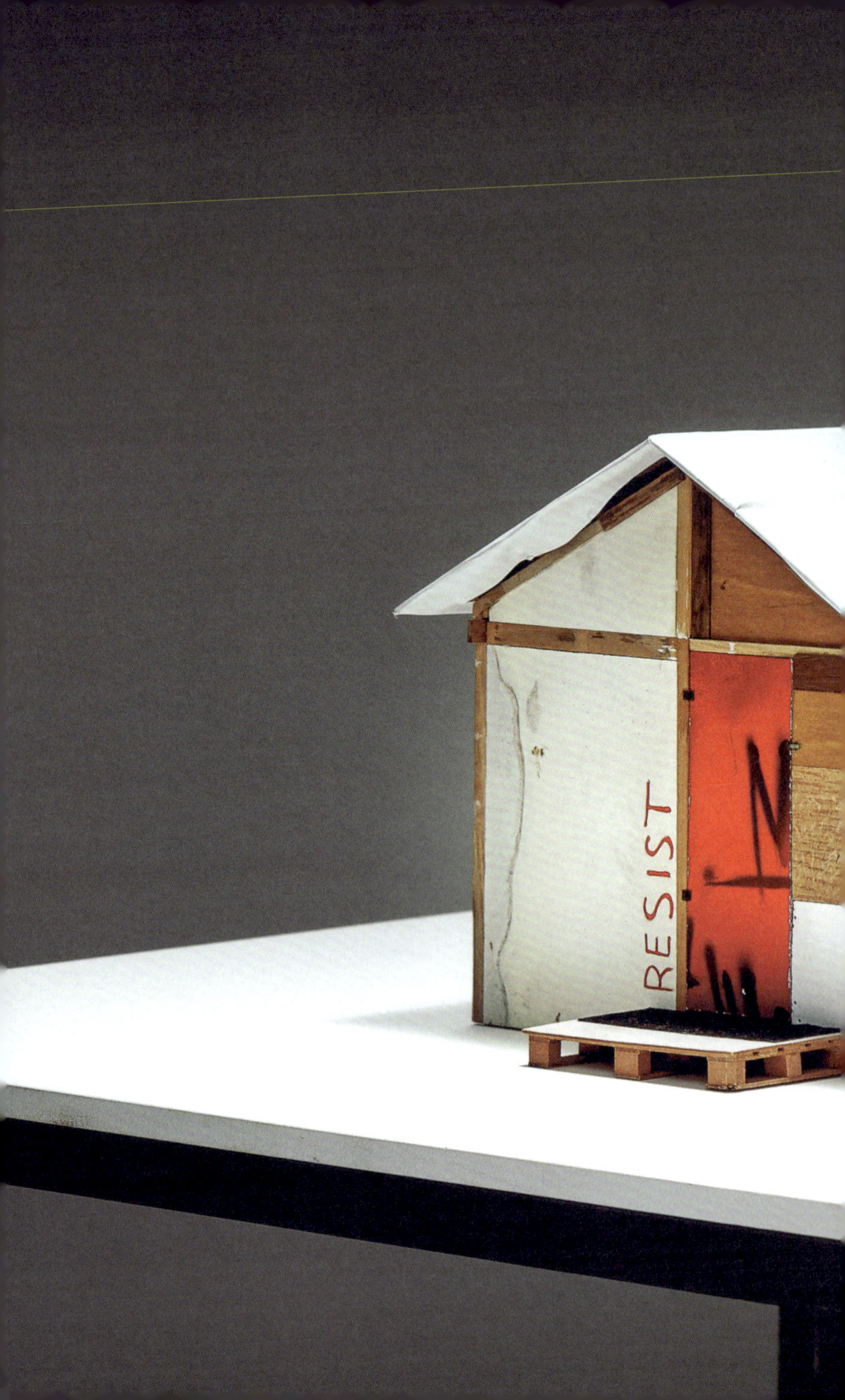
RESIST

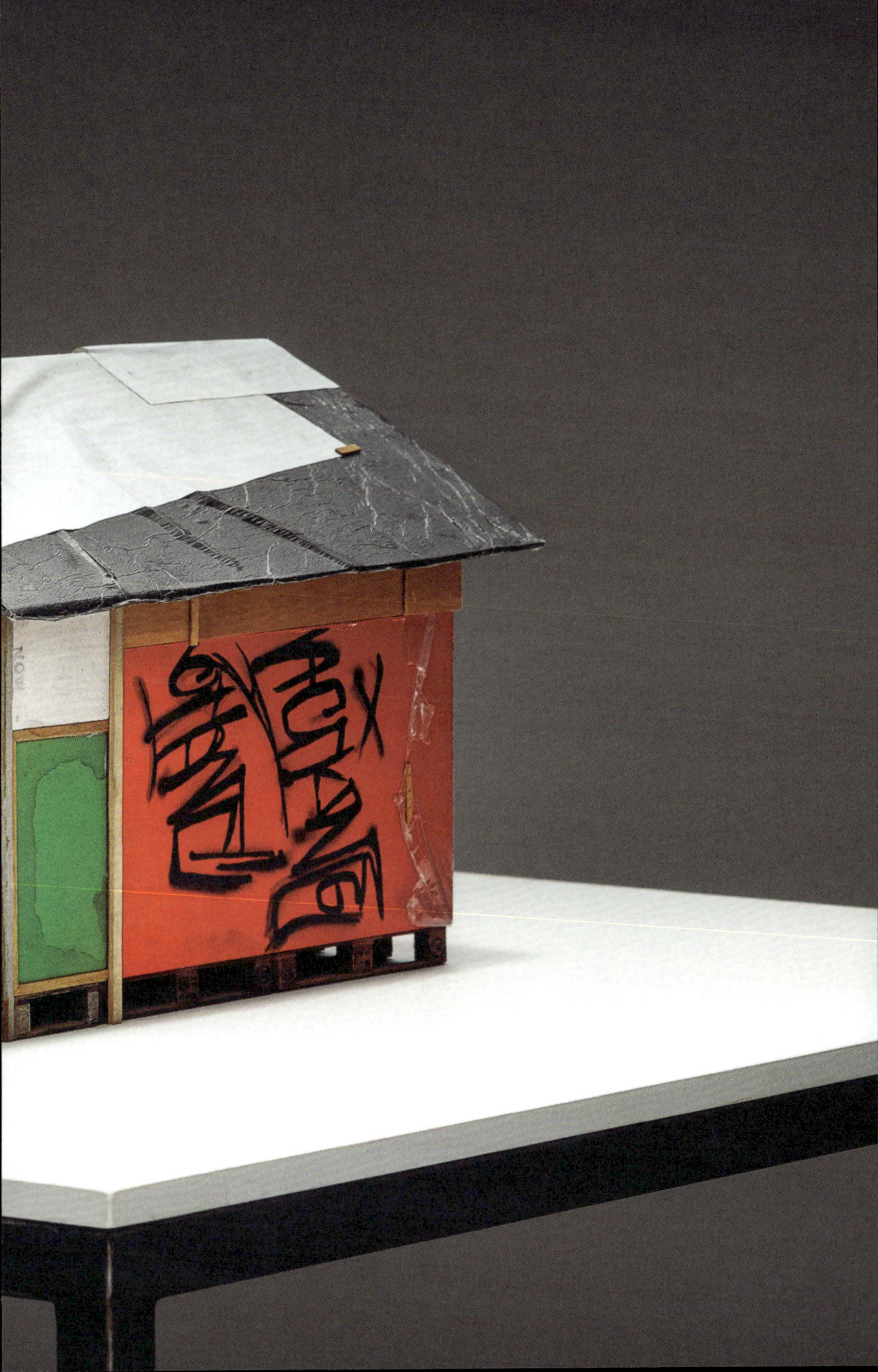

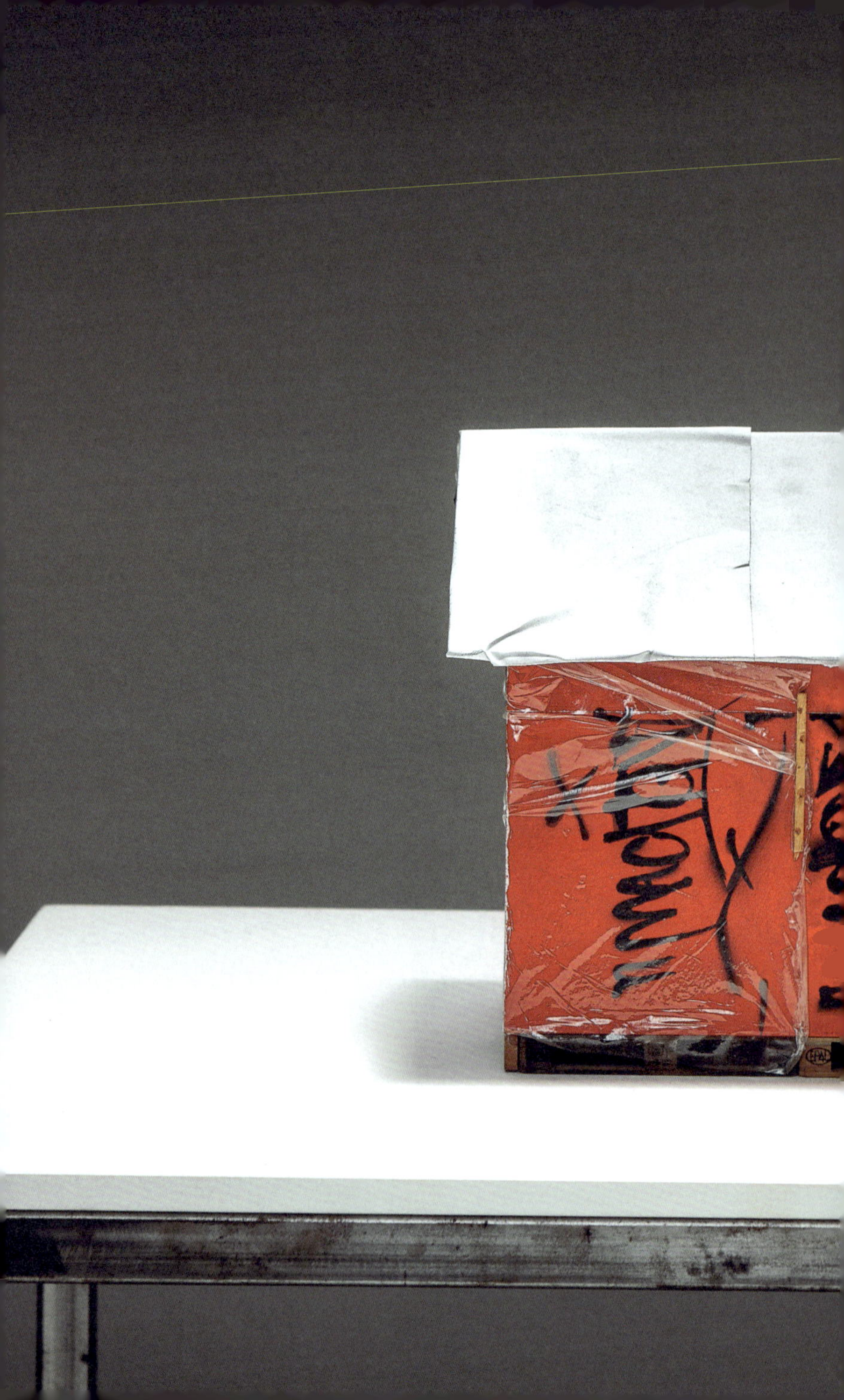

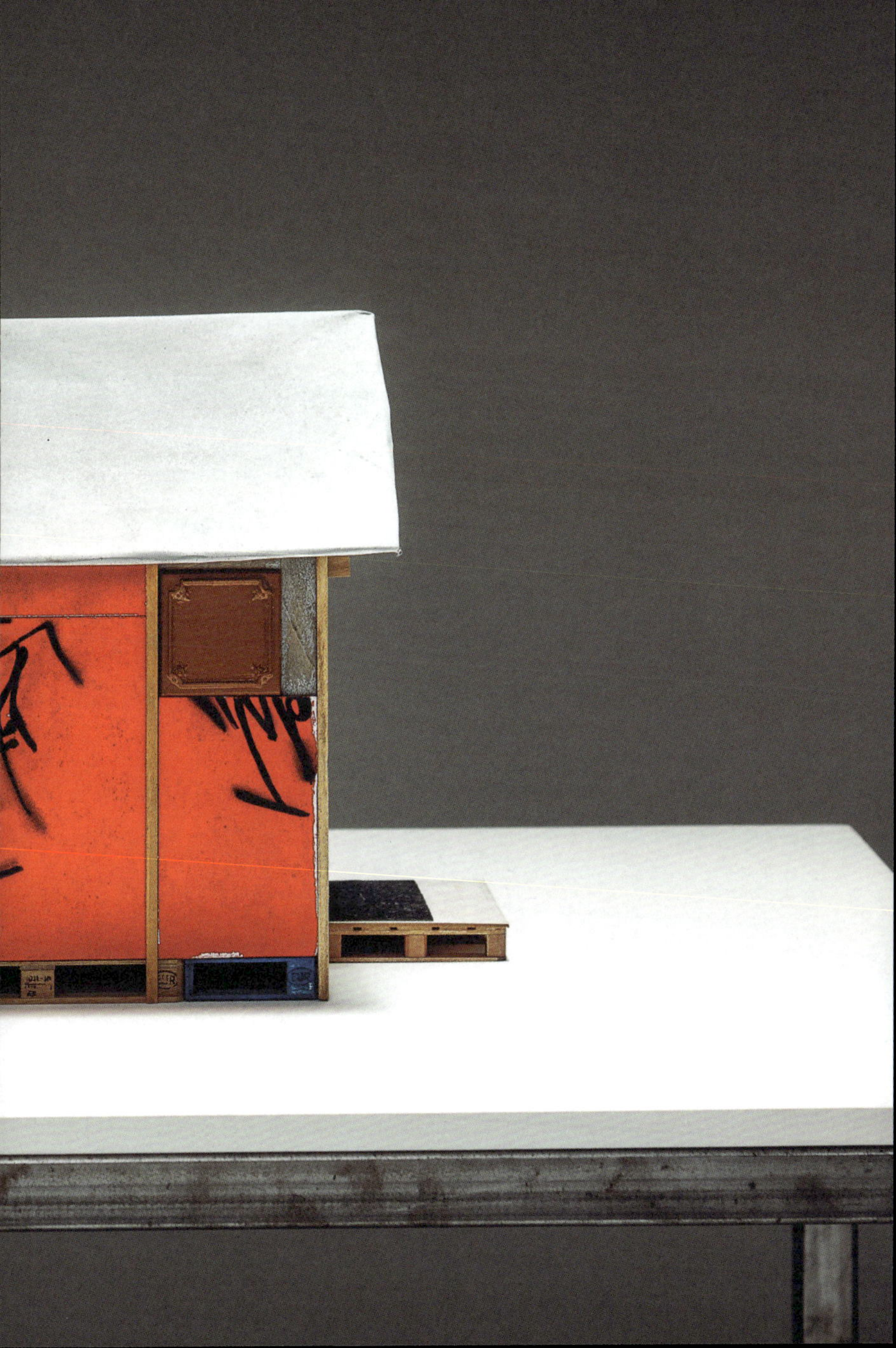

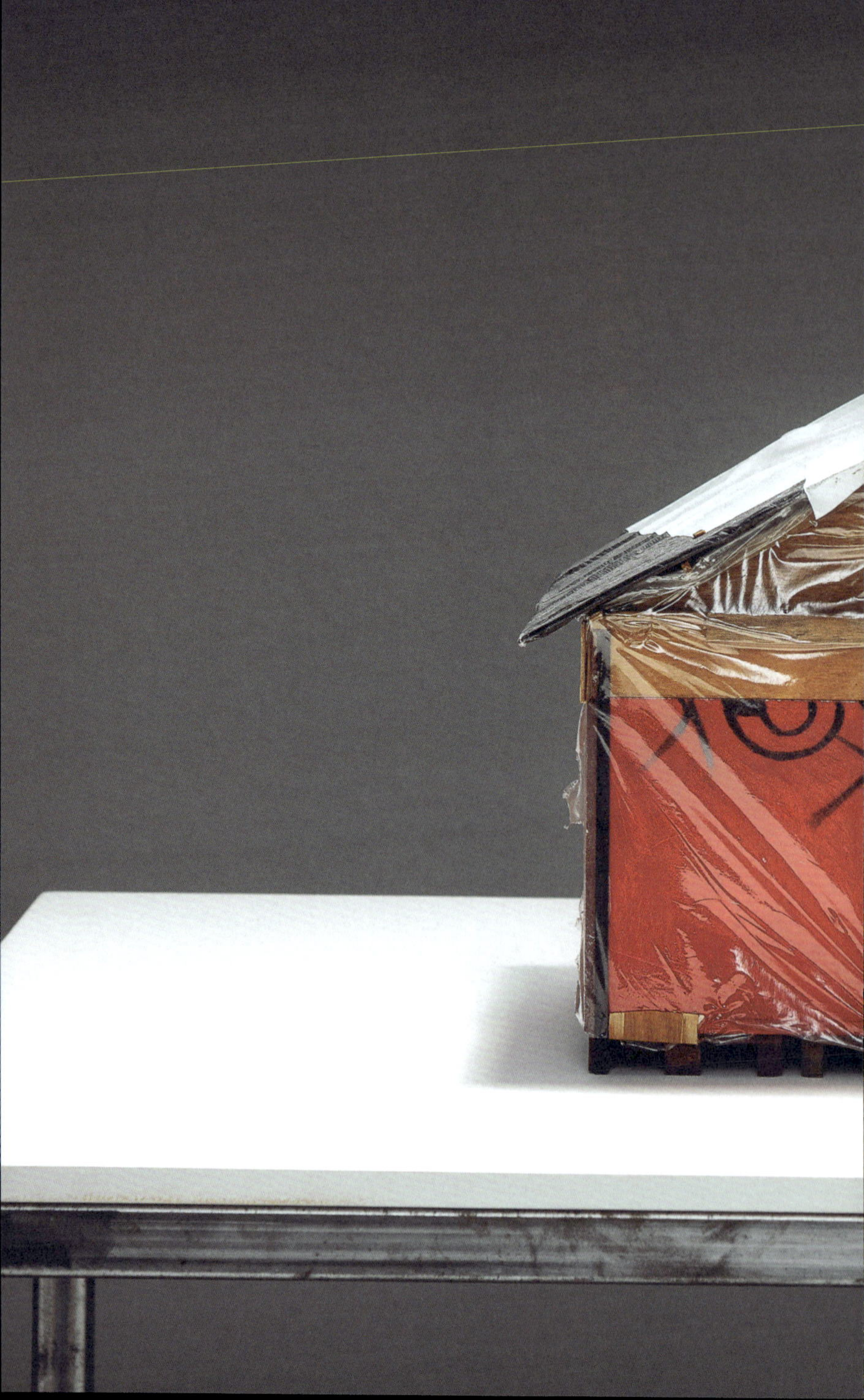

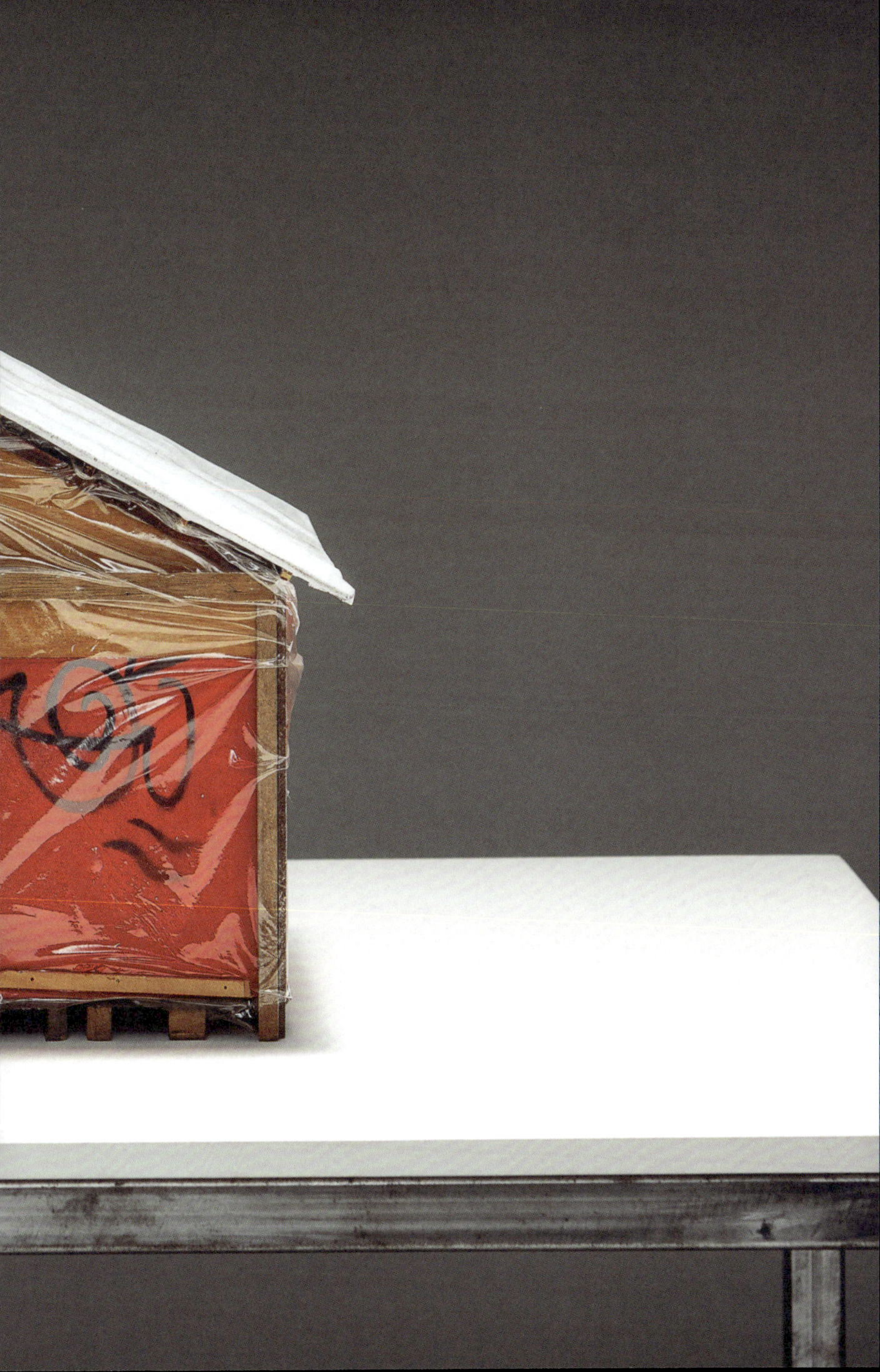

*Oranienplatz,* 2014

# D. Nomen
## *Mark von Schlegell*

> *Under ordinary conditions, this book is death or doom for the unsuspecting reader. Its title, author, date of publication must never, in any case, be spoken, written down or even glyphed. Furthermore, opening this volume at all while wearing even a shred of clothing will very likely occasion the reader's immanent demise. Secondly: reading this book in any light but firelight will very likely result in the reader's immediate death by strangulation.*

Not so strange in fact to be reading such a rarity in a windowless refugee's shack on the streets of Berlin. Ancient books are castaways like any other among those ripped by war and disaster. New technology has made it easier than ever to locate and advertise such singular volumes. Windowless was to the point. I was alone with enough flaming candles to read by. I took this book at its word, reading the unmentionable volume naked. And I felt strange indeed. Out of the protective polyethylene sleeve its current carrier kept it in, the white-skinned volume bared its devil signs starkly, pridefully tattooed with scarlet golden-edged type and sigil.

This edition told tales of the effects of earlier reprints, all up to today (1918). Tribute was paid to the printers, who were worked literally to death by the setting of the clearly demonic and perverse, but nonetheless somehow *sensical* letter-patterning. Explicitly blasphemous content obscured the deeper logic pattern within the 1d letter arrangement. Here, the possibility strings, when printed on any semi-organic material, even the animal cortex, when exposed to even the merest sunlight, *came to life*. Specific patterns revived ancient trojan horse bacteria, lethal when exposed by any light whose heat did not consume them. The poison appeared code-toxic in any translation.

I wanted something to cover myself with desperately. But a book, I remembered, can do many things. I held the death book forth as it were a shield and protection from itself. I was the first, and only reader; the leaves hadn't been opened. I had a silver knife, a ceremonial Etruscan dagger, remarkable for its broad, mirror-shining blade. I used it to deckle two pages at random, gently bringing to firelight a tale from the European 16th century.

The story concerned a great banquet on a saint's day. Your author hadn't known the situation had been so civilized already in the City-state of W., duchy of D. Servants of Lord C. in the Fort of D. had been slaughtering privately grown megafauna for a week now to serve the never-ending tour of gentles passing through the long-tabled hall. The attending smallfolk were lucky to be working. Many fed off of the trash and leavings periodically jettisoned from the Hall. Horrific suffering stalked the miserable beings beyond the sewage ditches surrounding the house. Drought had locals too weak to defend themselves. Bandits and self-proclaimed prophets raged through the burned-over district, leaving mud-thatched huts burning into air-corrupting flame. Crops withered; the poor huddled together in structures originally designed for the storage of perishables. Within the perimeter meanwhile, nothing disturbed my Lord and his banquet.

Every fine visitor had to pass in close proximity to the rabble. It was great amusement for the noblest visitors to poke the ribs of the poor with sticks as they approached the house. But one particular uninvited guest arrived on the seventh day, the unholy Sabbath of that riot. One guest proved much talked about ever since, whose raid is now the subject of this tale.

His appearance caused immediate interest. Unusual for such circles, it was clear that beneath his ill-fitting black topcoat, this man's upper portions were naked. A large hairy belly and two hairy breasts were clearly visible. His lower portions were covered more completely, but similarly awkwardly. The pantaloons were needlessly puffy, and the boots' sizes wrong. He was bald, save for two horn-like angles of smokey hair that swept back like ears. Black whiskers and beard did not obscure his scowl. Though not a tall man, he wore enormous black boots, the sort worn by those with club feet, of which he appeared to have two.

This strange-gaited specimen did not poke the children, nor the ancients as he passed. This was not because he bore them no ill will. To the contrary, the grimaces and snorting made it clear this was not the case. He simply preferred not to bother with such insects. He raised one right hand, and they scattered as if he'd thrown scalding liquid upon them. He walked with determination along the long refuse laden path to the gate, shuffling in great boots, leaning far forward on a thick ash cane. He progressed more rapidly than should have been possible, leaning far forward as if into the future, nimbly up the great stairs.

"Not a guest! D. Nomen?" He was reported to have

said various things. But all agree his hair and eye were smokey and black, and that in a brief struggle during which he disabled the butler with a blow from great forehead to face, he stumbled. This was when two guards grabbed him by the boots. These slipped greasily off the uninvited guest, the guards rolling and tumbling—revealing the hairy lower limbs of a goat.

Now as many of those outside, and some among the servants as well were full aware, it is an easy enough thing to trim and groom the hooves of a goat. But these horny feet showed rude and untrimmed, and it was clear to those who knew that the rot had set in.

"Yes indeed," he spoke, holing the scuncheon with a hoof. "D. Nomen's among ye."

He burst through the door of the great hall, coming upon a scene of such abandon that his entrance occurred unremarked upon. All along the great table lay strewn a heaping range of foodstuffs—newer meats, cheeses, and fruits decaying atop the rotting carcasses of meals gone past. Inebriated guests filled every place, engaged in furious activity of no purpose or inherent sense.

On any other such day my Lord would have had such an uninvited intruder speared, kept alive for the drawing, quartering, and gutting that he deserved. But today, down at end of the table by the great fire, our Lord remained fascinated by a book. A wicked book splayed whorishly open before him, concealing him from our view. It had taken his attention so long now, that the leg of lamb in his fist remained uneaten, and was in fact already alive with feasting flies. My Lord was more naked than the uninvited guest, only a slim robe of silk partially obscured his royal flesh.

Transfixed by the book's tales of its own wickedness, our Lord did not see the uninvited guest thrust swiftly forward, as if he meant to head-butt the near-end of the great table itself. As those about retreated in disorder, D. Nomen hopped up—a leap no man might have made similarly. He knocked down sixty-six wooden goblets when he landed, spilling much juice, saliva, and mead, overturning soups and sauces in the process. He strode with great hairy muscular legs, roughly along that wooden stage, laughing, leaping, flinging jellies, meats and head-cheeses. At last he came to table's end. Here, after leap-kick, rotation and final tumble, he exploded in an electrically-charged nimbus—exactly before the seat of my Lord.

When the sulfurous obscurity had cleared, D. Nomen was nowhere to be seen. It appeared that the devil disappeared into a crack in the book's spine. Upon further investigation it was discovered (by soon-to-be deceased detectives) that my blue-lipped Lord was not still reading. He was dead. It is sometimes so hard to tell the difference.

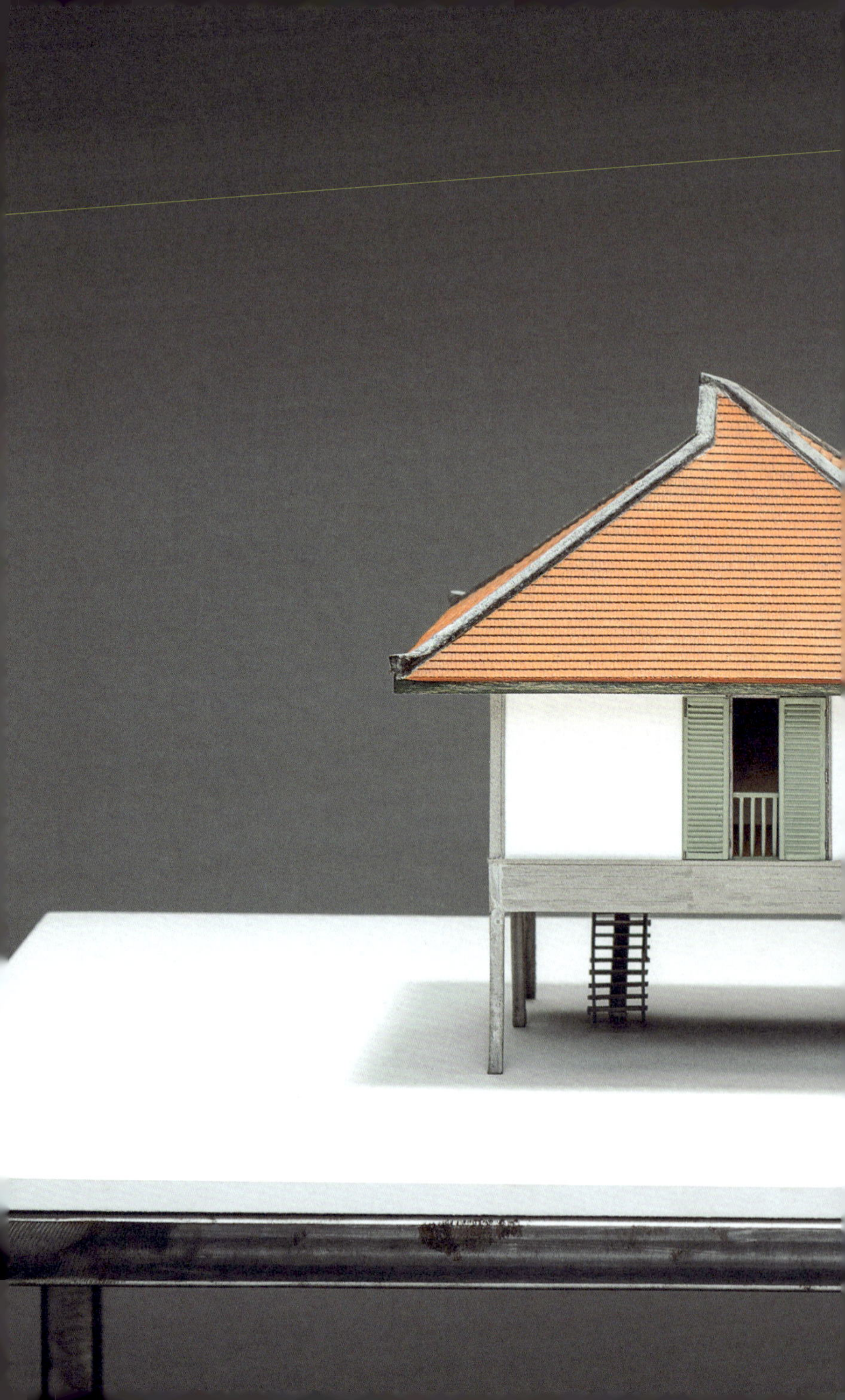

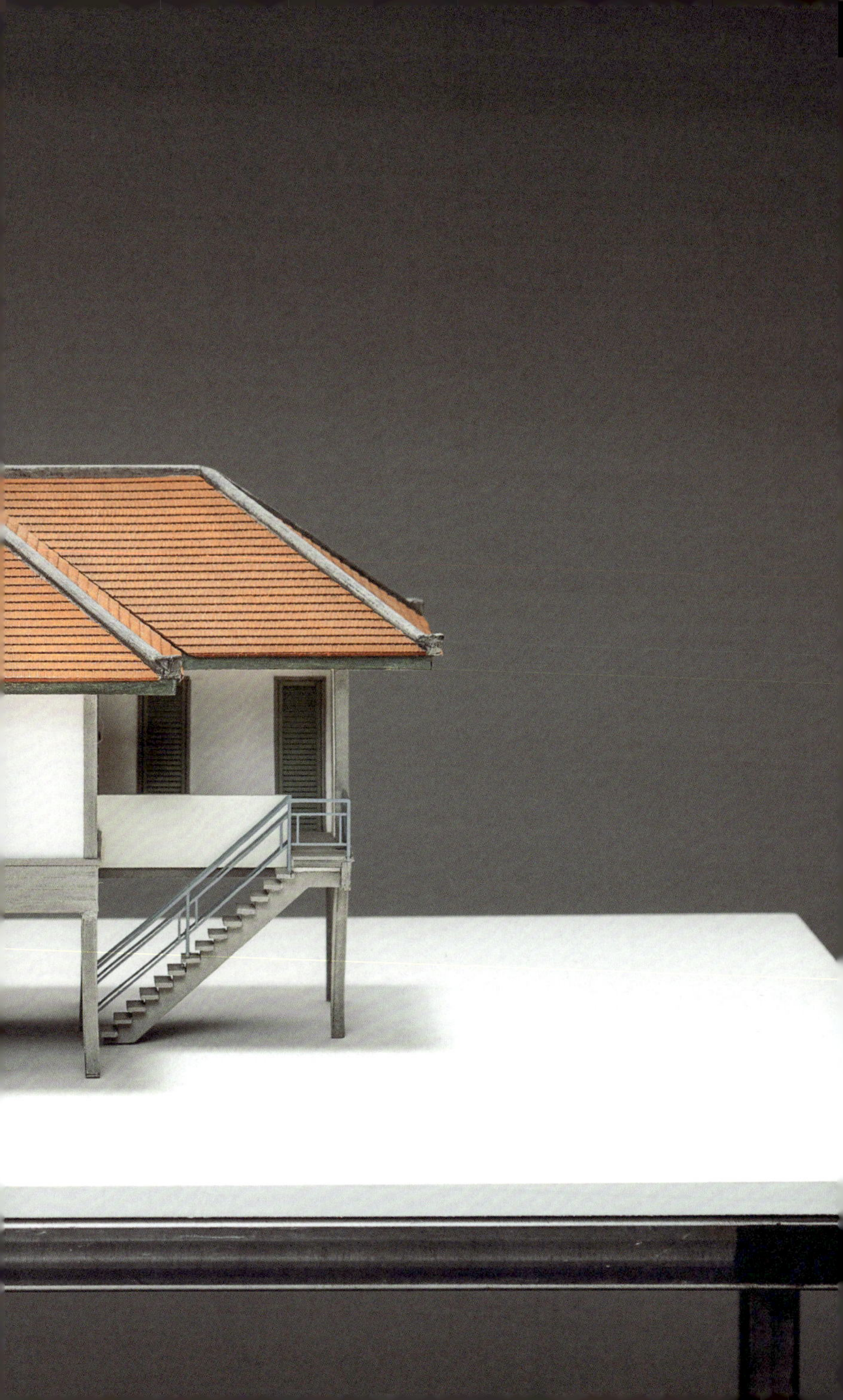

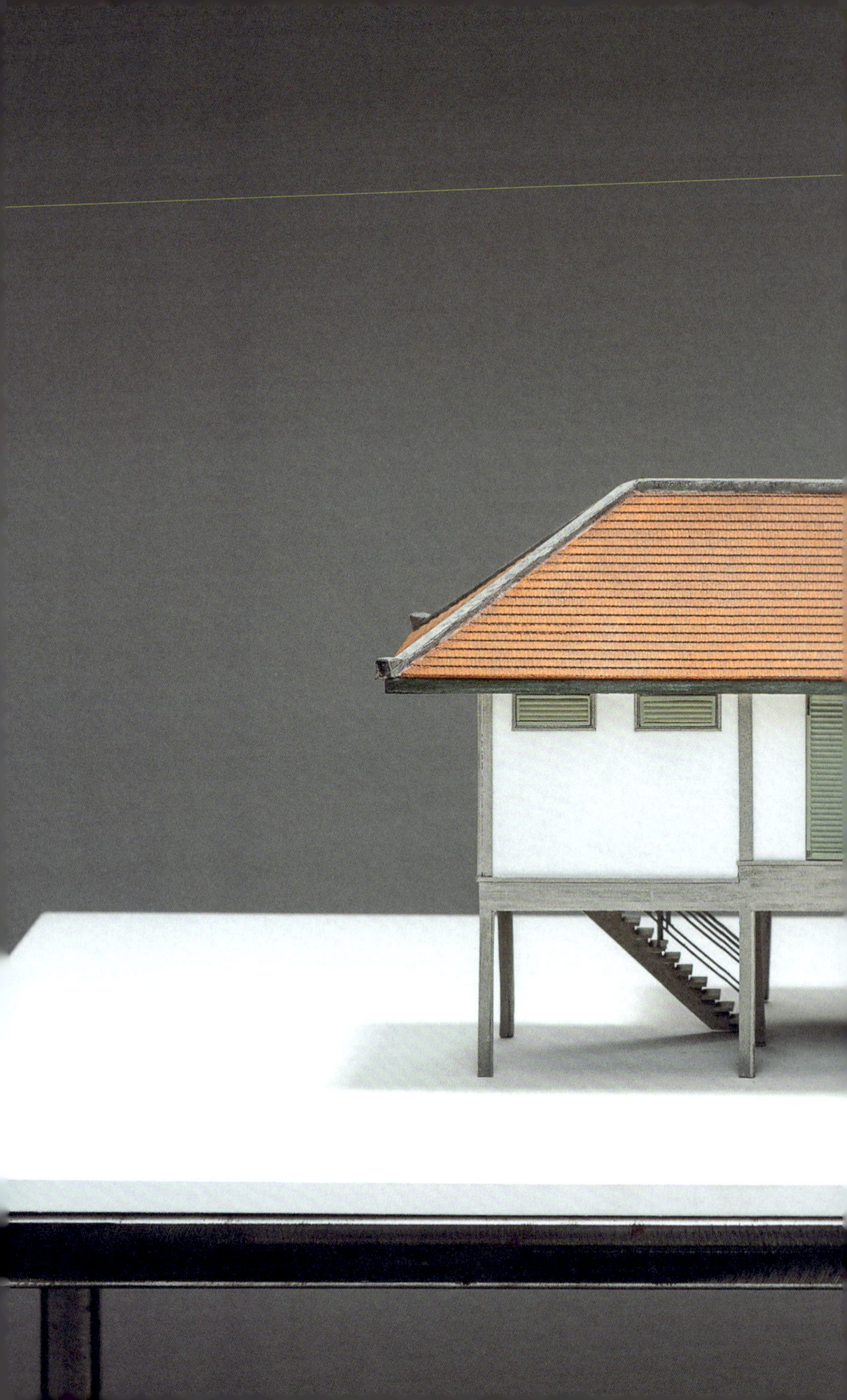

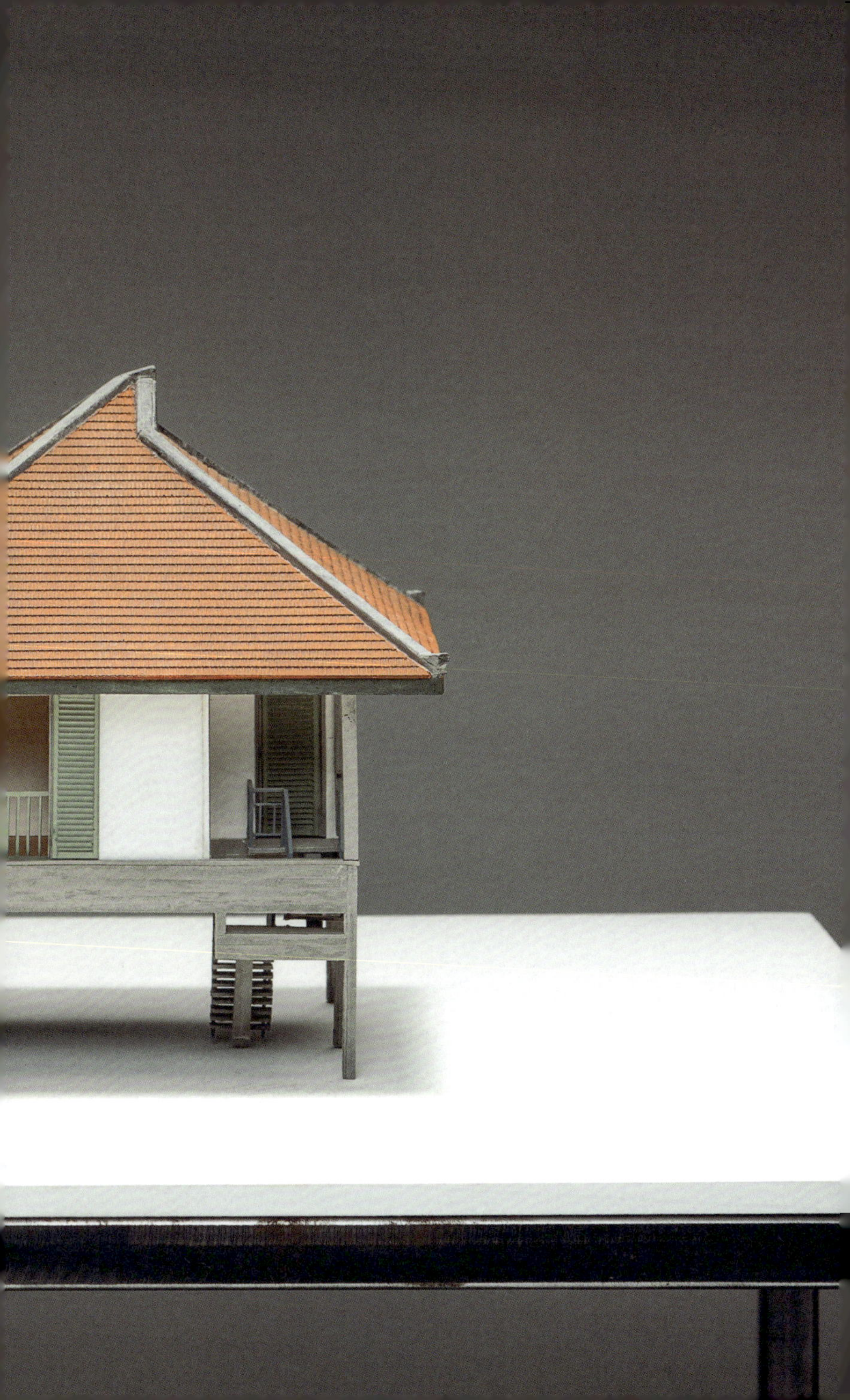

*101*, 2016

# One Hundred Government Clerks (A Mockup)

## *Attila Bartis*

One hundred government clerks are going home. All the same direction. They're all named K., let's say, though they don't know that. They're all wearing white, button-down shirts, let's say, and black overcoats, so they look exactly how we tend to imagine government clerks look. They should match precisely the image conjured by a mid-range imagination. And let's say it's pouring down rain, but they're prepared, they all have umbrellas. And they should put them down on the porch. All one hundred K.s should enter the one hundred dwellings without a spot or splash of dirt on them. And they should have their monthly salaries in their pockets.

At home, a hundred wives should be waiting for them, with three or four children per family. They should glance at the youngest child and see in him the distant future. The distant future, of course, should be beyond reach, improbable, almost impossible. I.e. it should be beautiful and good and just. They should ask the middle child whether their fever has gone down. The oldest should be studying to be an attorney so that someday they will accomplish the many things that K. came so close to accomplishing, just something always came up, a child or a fever or a parent's desires. Something, it little matters what. Something that made it impossible, in the end, to get any higher than the offices on the ground floor. But this should be a good thing. The pressure on the oldest shouldn't be a burden, and their aspirations should not fall unrealistically far from the actual opportunities, or their parents' wishes.

One of the children should be a little girl, and the little girl should be learning to be a good wife someday, but in her heart of hearts she should long to be a French movie star. She should know a few French songs, but she should be ashamed of herself for knowing them. And she should know that when she's about sixteen years old she will sing them for the last time. Then, later, perhaps she will sing them again to her children, but she will take care to be sure her husband doesn't hear. In a word, she should be preparing to assume the safest role for a woman. A respectable Khmer woman doesn't sing French songs anyway. That is what the daughter should be thinking when K. enters the home. She should watch closely and attentively to learn how a proper wife helps her husband take off his overcoat. Then she should watch as they divide his salary into useful groups after dinner. Money for food and upkeep of the house, for school, for clothing, and of course savings. When they go to bed, the wife should take the initiative, or she should at least be responsive to his initiative. They should be happy.

There is nothing scandalous, nothing false. All one hundred K.s can be happy. Or at least content. Of course, they may sometimes feel a bit dissatisfied. They may think the room is a bit cramped, the bathroom a mess, the homework unfinished, the news on the radio troubling. Just dissatisfied enough not to get dead drunk and sleep through the remaining sixteen hours until morning the following day. But all in all, they should be happy. Or at least content. They should be comforted to know that they belong to the middle class, and no one can take that away from them. Except God and death.

The alarm should go off at six o'clock, and at seven o'clock the coffee should perk, and the radio should be playing the news. The bank should open at eight. And the next day too and one year later too. After a few years, K. should get a divorce. Or not a divorce yet, he should just go out somewhere and have a cup of tea. And after his first tea excursion, he should smack the kids around. One government clerk out of a hundred. That's within reason, within the limits. Perhaps he should screw a whore. His wife should cry, she should say it's not true. Then she should find the bits of tea leaves that he put in the pocket of his overcoat as a memento. She should go to every last one of the ninety-nine stilt houses, she should want to have a cup of tea in each one, she should steal a pinch of the tea leaves and compare them with the unimaginable tea leaves that she found in her husband's pocket. She should cry for months, and she should have nightmares every night. Once, when she hears her daughter singing a French song, she too should strike her.

K. is clearly no longer happy. He may even make mistakes in his work at the office. But his colleagues realize in time, they discuss it, compute the percentages again, fix the mistakes. The figures are correct again. In the end, he should decide that he will not get a divorce after all, because divorce is neither ethical nor practical. At home, he only rarely speaks to his wife, and when he speaks to the children, it is only to rebuke them. The youngest child admits that for months now they have not wanted to be a scientist who studies space. The oldest has been accepted to the law school, and the girl's husband is emphatically not an existentialist film director. All in all, K. still has no reason to doubt that, while he may not be happy and, indeed, he probably never was happy, he belongs to the middle class. And no one can take that away from him. Except God and death.

In a word, K. should be the paragon. The embodiment of the ideal. Like his family, his home, the housing development for government clerks. There are many such developments. Almost every decent city has made a housing development for its clerks. Târgu Mureș, Budapest, Berlin. Maybe even New York. Delhi for sure. In Yogyakarta, it wasn't the bank that built nice, almost Javanese dwellings, all the same shape and size, on inexpensive land for its clerks, but the sugar factory. In Budapest, it was Prime Minister Wekerle himself. And he gave the rising Hungarian middle class more than just one thousand residences. He also gave them churches, schools, and a police station. And how very right he was to do so.

It doesn't matter whether it's along the banks of the Seine or the Danube or the Mekong. Where a bourgeois middle class is beginning to emerge, one must ask an architect to build on tradition, on practical considerations, and on aesthetics, but first and foremost on cost-effectiveness. Be modern, but keep in mind the peculiarities of the human soul too, which the so-called modern has not always managed to do. And build one hundred houses all the same shape and size. Possibly several thousand.

But for the moment let's forget the housing development in Târgu Mureș, where my mother's mother was driven mad by fear when the communists came, and let's forget the development in Budapest too, where my children's mother's mother shed tears of joy when the communists came. Let's forget the housing developments for the government clerks which had been rid of Jews, of Hungarians, of bourgeois.

Let's even forget the housing developments no one ever wanted to move in to. Let's forget the developments built for government clerks in China, which were based on Western models and in which the Chinese government clerks showed no interest, thus the English ghost town next to Shanghai, complete with klinker-brick buildings, red telephone booths, and a Shakespeare statue, can easily be turned over to young couples who do not yet have enough money to go to London for their honeymoons so that they can use it as a backdrop in their wedding pictures.

We should focus on the one hundred stilt houses in Phnom Penh. It should be morning, the coffee should just have perked. The radio should be playing the news. One hundred men in black, button-down shirts should be walking down the main street. Ninety-nine of them should not know how to read or write, not as if anyone's sense of justice had anything to do with knowledge or books. One of them should have a middle-class family background, and he should have dropped out of the school in Paris before graduating. He should have a completely viable vision of the future. The future should be beautiful and good and just. So he too should have a sense of justice.

They should all knock at once on the doors to one hundred stilt houses, and they should all sit down on the kitchen stools at the same time and pull the coffee away from K. and towards themselves. They should stir in the sugar, and they should ask K. to turn off the radio, the news it is reporting is no longer valid. They should explain to K.'s wife that she needn't worry herself over K.'s salary, because from now on no one will need a salary, everyone will make what they need for the kitchen table themselves. K. should have some objection to this, but he should not dare voice it. He should only think it. In response, the man should say that he is wrong. The man should have the middle child, whose fever has just gone down, and the older child, who was just accepted to law school, sit down next to K. He should ask K. where his daughter is. He should find it regrettable that she has married. He should explain that relations between a man and a woman are not a matter for the individual to decide.

He should give a wave of his arm to indicate to the youngest child that he should come over and take a seat in his lap. He should show him the magazine, and the two of them should count the cartridges. He should explain that cartridges are very expensive, and they have to be divided up and put to good use as attentively as the money for food and upkeep of the house. He should also explain, very clearly and logically, why there is no need for K. or for more attorneys or for someone who is always running a fever. Together, they should turn off the safety and take aim.

And once we're done with all this, once we have imagined what we have never been able to imagine in time, or if we were, then we never had a useful answer, once we are past the yes, yes, but this is all quite unimaginable here, on the banks of the Seine or the Elba or the Danube, because we are past all that, once we have thought everything through, have checked and rechecked all the odds and percentages, once we have rebuilt all the stilt houses that once stood along the banks of the Mekong, once the attendants in the museum watch carefully to be sure we don't touch the perforated skulls, then we can go back and start at the beginning again. One hundred government clerks are going home. All the same direction.

# The Invisible Ocean
## *Mike Wilson*

A decade has passed since Roque took over the house, an abandoned cabin atop a hill overlooking the Pacific. He hadn't been a young man when he disembarked, now he is elderly. He'd left the cove behind and climbed the hill not knowing where he was going. He saw a neglected house, the grass overgrown, the window panes broken. He found the door unlocked, went inside, and stayed.

He came to the ocean to wait for death. He had reached old age alone, and he wanted to await the end calmly, surrender as to a deep sleep, freed from the dreary procession of days. By then he knew who he was, and the stillness had taken firm root in him. Now, he no longer agonizes over things that used to keep him up at night and everything is simpler, he doesn't feel the need to resolve anything, there was never any need and now he understands that.

The blindness started about eight or nine months ago. First he noticed that the normal shine of things had dimmed, as if the days were always cloudy. He didn't give it much importance, even convinced himself that the former luminosity of the world was a trick of his memory, that things had never really been like that.

He lives with a dog who showed up on its own, big and black with a blue tongue. He didn't name it—the dog was already grown and he felt like giving it a name at this point would be to wrest away another name that he didn't know.

To be alone now, as things are ending, is a relief. There's no one to fake it for, no reason to fake it, he can be nobody and not pretend to be someone. Roque always felt exhausted by that aspect of being around other people, the pressure of having to dress up as someone, to act like he was someone, a someone invented so as not to make others uncomfortable with his emptiness. Now he finally feels he can leave that playacting behind and rest. There's a small triumph in that, to reach death knowing he is with himself, free of noise, of dependency.

In the afternoons, the fog rises up from the ocean and the cold sets in. His routine is always the same: When the shadows lengthen and the cold mounts, he goes out to get firewood from the store on the terrace under an impermeable tarp. He takes three sheets of newspaper and the wooden bench and sits in front of the fireplace. He arranges the logs over crumpled paper and then sets fire to it. He can still perceive the light of the flames, a weak shine, sometimes yellowish, other times tinged with red. He lets the newspaper burn until he hears the wood crackle, until he smells the burnt pine and feels the heat on his face. The dog stays with him, attentive to his every step. The animal lies down with his face toward the fireplace and lets himself be warmed.

In the mornings, he delays the moment of getting up. Sometimes, at dawn, he thinks of himself as a sad man. He fears waking up; there is something violent about the amnesia of sleep and the recurring epiphany that one inhabits a heavy world in a heavy body, as if gravity didn't apply during sleep.

A few months back he stopped seeing himself in the mirror. No matter how close he got to the surface of the glass, it returned nothing more than a blurry smudge. Nor could he see other people's faces now—they had also become smudges. He was astonished at how quickly one can forget the contours of a face. He can't even call up his own features. An abstraction, perhaps, but he can't recall the details, the exact outline of his cheekbones, the shape of his eyes, the arch of his brows, all nuances have been lost for good.

When he finally gets out of bed he heads straight for the bathroom, the floorboards creaking under his feet. He goes in and steadies himself, rests his hand on the wall while he urinates. It's a slow affair, but Roque is patient. He thinks of the ocean, squeezes his eyelids shut and assembles the image. He may not remember faces but he has retained the ocean—it appears to him in detail, the waves, the white crests, the foam and the savage, unfathomable breathing of the depths. He recognizes the relief that comes with the final trickle. He buttons up and leaves, finds the dog waiting in the hallway.

The pain comes at night. At first it was only a slight aggravation, but it wasn't long before the ache sharpened and began to wake him in the early morning hours. He felt like his eyes were going to burst, and a stabbing agony pierced his head. Each night, he allowed himself to scream in the darkness. No one would hear, there were no other houses nearby and the ocean would drown his keening. Only the dog heard the old man's torture, and suffered and howled along with him.

The dog knows when he is in pain, and he comes over and rests his head on Roque's chest, licks his chin. Roque lets him, doesn't hide his agony from the animal—only with him can he let himself cry. He knows the dog doesn't judge him, only loves him. He cries without qualms, without self-reproach, it's the only use he has left for his eyes.

After lunch he turns on the radio and opens the door to the terrace to let in a little air. He feels a breeze and hears the whisper of grass blowing. He settles in on the bench in front of the fireplace, slaps his knee a few times, and the dog comes. The radio isn't clear, the frequency is intermittent, the announcer is just a hissing voice saying something about a storm approaching. It recommends taking measures, boarding up the windows, not leaving loose objects out in the open. A little while later the breeze becomes wind, the wooden door slams against the planks of the cabin's wall, the tarp over the firewood flaps furiously. He goes out to sniff the air; it smells metallic, and is unblemished by the barking of seals or the seagulls' calls. He perceives a change in the light, a dark blot that spreads out from the horizon and extinguishes the sky, speeding closer over the ocean, reaching the cove and climbing the hill to swallow everything.

There had been one night when he'd woken up thirsty, his mouth dry and his tongue swollen, and he got up to get some water. He took two steps and tripped, head against the bed frame, and he blacked out. He woke up to the dog's whine. The animal was lying beside him, licking the blood from his forehead. He stayed lying on the floorboards, hugging the dog to him. He breathed deeply and again pictured the ocean. He saw it absolutely, as if he were standing there on the terrace looking out over the railing. The infinite grey sea, a timeless leviathan that expanded and crashed against the rocks with a thunderous roar. It shook his chest, he felt the tide in his belly, the cold and invisible ocean inside the house, there with him, always with him.

Now, the storm is approaching. The wind blows fast and the ocean bellows. Roque feels his way across the terrace in search of the boards he keeps to cover the windows. The cold air makes his fingers go numb. It's only five in the afternoon but the light is grey and it's hard for him to distinguish silhouettes. The clouds are dense and everything below seems muted.

Happiness is not a thing Roque is after. He only wants to be calm, to feel peace, to make the most of that final stillness that cannot be rushed or faked, a privilege for those who are on the threshold and can discern the twilight. Only there, in that singular place, can the yoke lighten and tranquility descend like a warm blanket. His bones ache, blindness deprives him, but things are already determined and the agonies that come have arrived very late, condemned to a brevity that strips them of anguish.

The grey clouds over the sea light up, the blaze of lightning flashes so bright that for an instant Roque sees clearly. The light is etched into his retinas and he can observe the silhouette of all he cannot see, the ocean's outline, and it's a way of seeing without seeing, observing the texture of the enormous waves, the foam spewed up toward the sky, the swollen guts of a black ocean.

The thunder comes soon after, deep and low. He stands still, the wind inflating his jacket and blowing his hair, and he feels the rumble in the marrow of his bones. The dog barks and whines, then darts away to hide under the sofa.

He finds the boards, hoists one up, it's heavy, he holds a couple of nails between his teeth, the wind shakes everything, he tries to hold the plank steady against the window, raises the hammer, brings it down on his fingers. He drops the board. He can't, he can't. He collapses to the ground, exhausted by the effort and frustrated by his own impotence. He can't take anymore, and he covers his face with his hands. The dog leaves his hiding place and leans against Roque.

The gale converges on the coast and spins like a colossal motor, a gear that builds strength and tenses the inner workings of the storm. Catastrophe swirls within it, electric and chaotic, it illuminates the sea.

The rain starts to pelt Roque and the dog, and the air turns completely black. Roque gets up from the boards and goes inside the cabin. He struggles to close the terrace door against the wind. The dog barks furiously at the emptiness as if he were going to scare off the lightning. The wind wins out and the door throws the old man to the floor; the flames in the fireplace jump. The horizontal rain enters the house, the door beats harder and shakes everything as if it were the blows of a furious beast brought by the thunderstorm. Roque stays lying on the floor, the dog barks and barks, the rain soaks both of them and extinguishes the fire.

He squeezes his eyelids again, ignoring the rain that bores into his skin, and he imagines the ocean. He sees it in all its glory, every wave, every crest, he pictures the seaweed piled up on the beach, the jellyfish deposited on the sand, he observes the bubbles that rise up from the bottom of the abyss. He sees it, sees the ocean as he never could before.

The storm charges at the coast, the cabin trembles, the windows shatter, the gale enters and Roque's ears pop, everything creaks, the zinc on the roof starts to peel off, he hears the metallic groan and the impact of the sheeting against the back patio fence. The squall stirs the inside of the house, topples the table, the chairs, the roof opens up and water falls from the sky. He gets up from the wet rug and takes the dog by the scruff of his neck. He leans his head into the wind and fights against the gust to head toward the terrace. The dog lets himself be led.

The storm surrounds him. Amid the fog, the rain and the lightning, the only thing he manages to see are hints of the flashing light. In his mind they appear like curtains of bright white that dissolve into red and blue shades. The flares are followed by the detonation of thunder that pounds in his ears. The dog sticks close to Roque, aware the old man needs him. Roque keeps his fingers on the animal's back and fumbles his way down the terrace stairs to the path that descends to the beach. He stumbles along in the mud against the wind and the rain, guides himself by dragging his knuckles along the wooden railing that edges the path. He hears a crash coming from the house, the destruction of metal and glass, splintering wood, it groans like a protracted collision. It's the sound of the house coming uprooted and tumbling violently down the hill toward the cliff. The dog never stops barking.

The ocean inflates along the coast as if an invisible wall were containing it at the beach. Rubble and branches fly through the air. A blackout stretches toward the interior, expanding like a shock wave, sections of landscape extinguished in procession.

He reaches the edge of the beach, feels the wet sand under his feet. He continues toward the ocean until he senses its immensity a few meters away, his body feeling the sea's colossal gravity. He straightens up and lets the gale blow furiously against him, his jacket fluttering, the stinging rain hitting his face, and he opens his mouth and tastes the storm. He hears the dog digging in the sand, digging in a frenzy.

Amid the groaning of the storm he hears the sounds of the world collapsing behind him. A grove of cypress trees is torn from the earth, the squall hacks them to pieces, he hears the cacophony of the small amusement park adjacent to the beach on the other side of the cove. The Ferris wheel and the mechanical games are toppled and the rubble rolls in a crash toward the hills like murderous motors. He hears the muffled smash of the wooden boats piling up against the pier, the broken and splintered wood.

He hallucinates that the storm is a destroying angel bringing ruin, that he is standing on the edge, on the dark border of the world, while all is obliterated behind him. He feels like a prophet raising the ocean to the skies. The dog goes on digging frantically in the sand.

Near the coast the swell gathers up the sea, lighting flashes illuminate the marine beasts. It's a different world under the water. Beneath there is calm and silence, no sign of the chaos storming in the sky save for the mute glow that descends to the abyss.

The dog stops digging and lies down exhausted at the bottom of the hole, in the water of a salty puddle. Roque feels his stillness, falls to the sand and crawls over to the edge of the hole. Between lightning and thunder he hears the dog's whine. He lets himself slide in and curls up with the dog, both of them nestled together in the small trench.

The dog trembles in his arms and Roque whispers to him while he squeezes his eyes shut and sees the ocean, sees it in full, majestic and terrible, sees every contour and surge, sees the calm that is there in the abyss, a timeless, eternal quietude. He also feels the strength that lifts up the waters, mountains of ocean built there on the shore, on top of him and the ruins of the world. He sees the beauty of the wave, his eyes penetrate the surface as if it were a diaphanous veil. This is what he came for. He cowers before the immense swell, the wave hangs in the night, hesitates above them for a second, above them and the entire coast. He breathes deeply, tightens his arms around the dog, contains its trembling and covers its eyes with his hand.

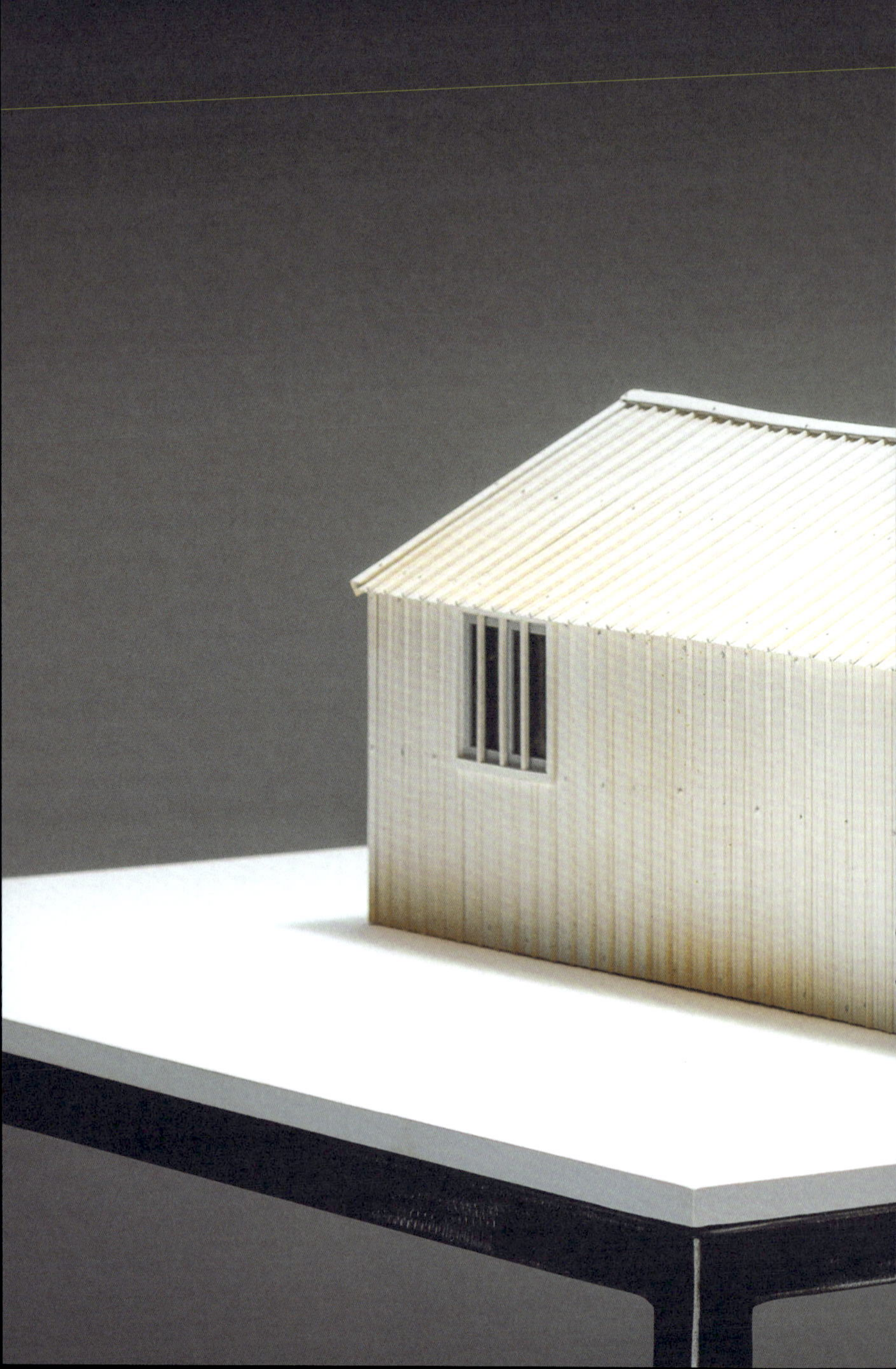

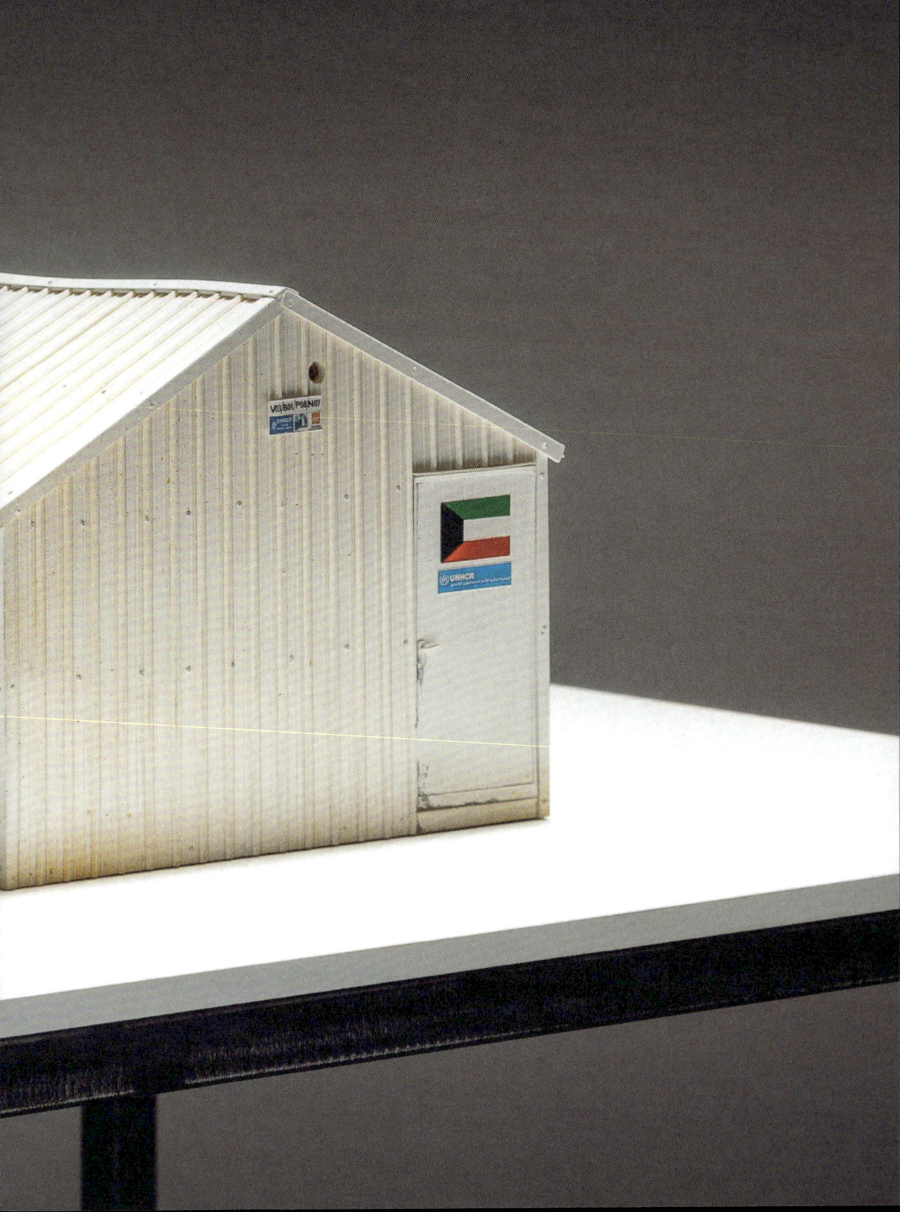
UNHCR

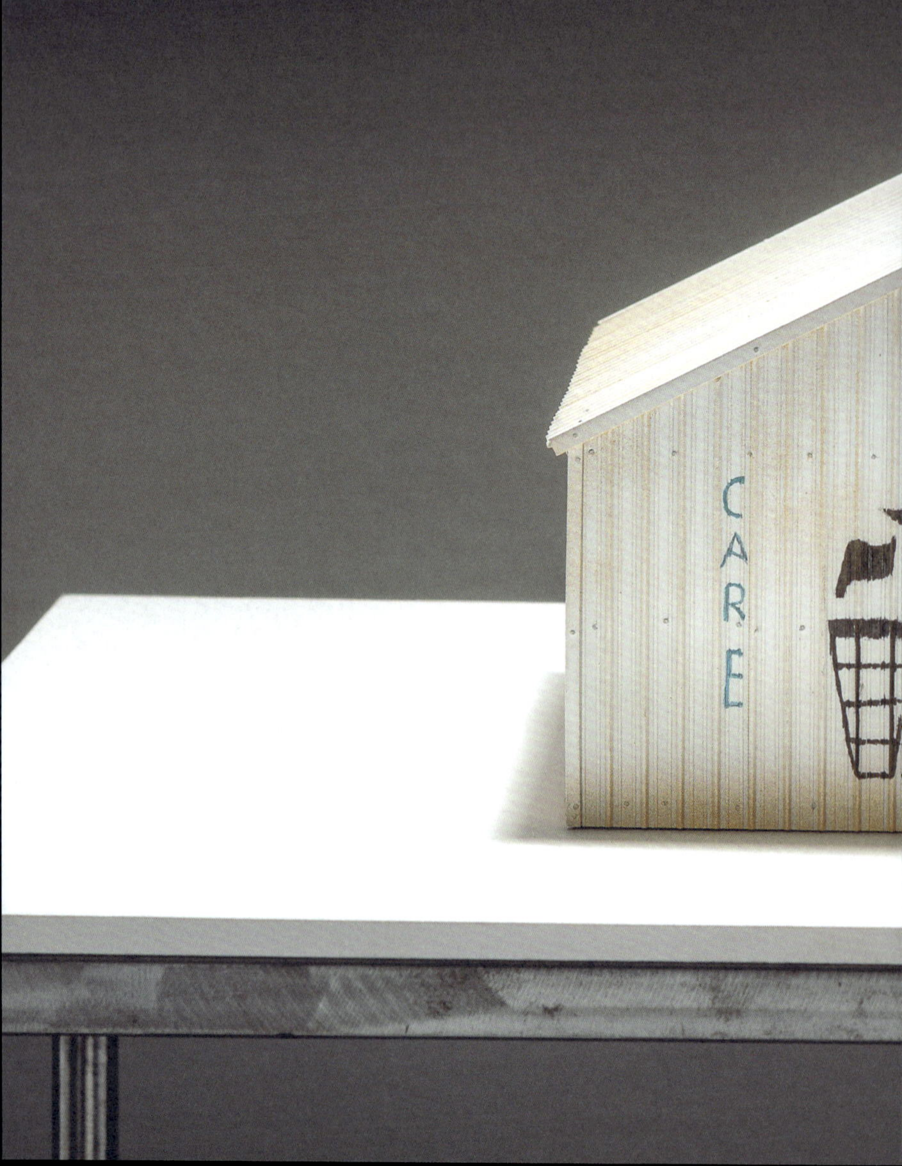
CARE

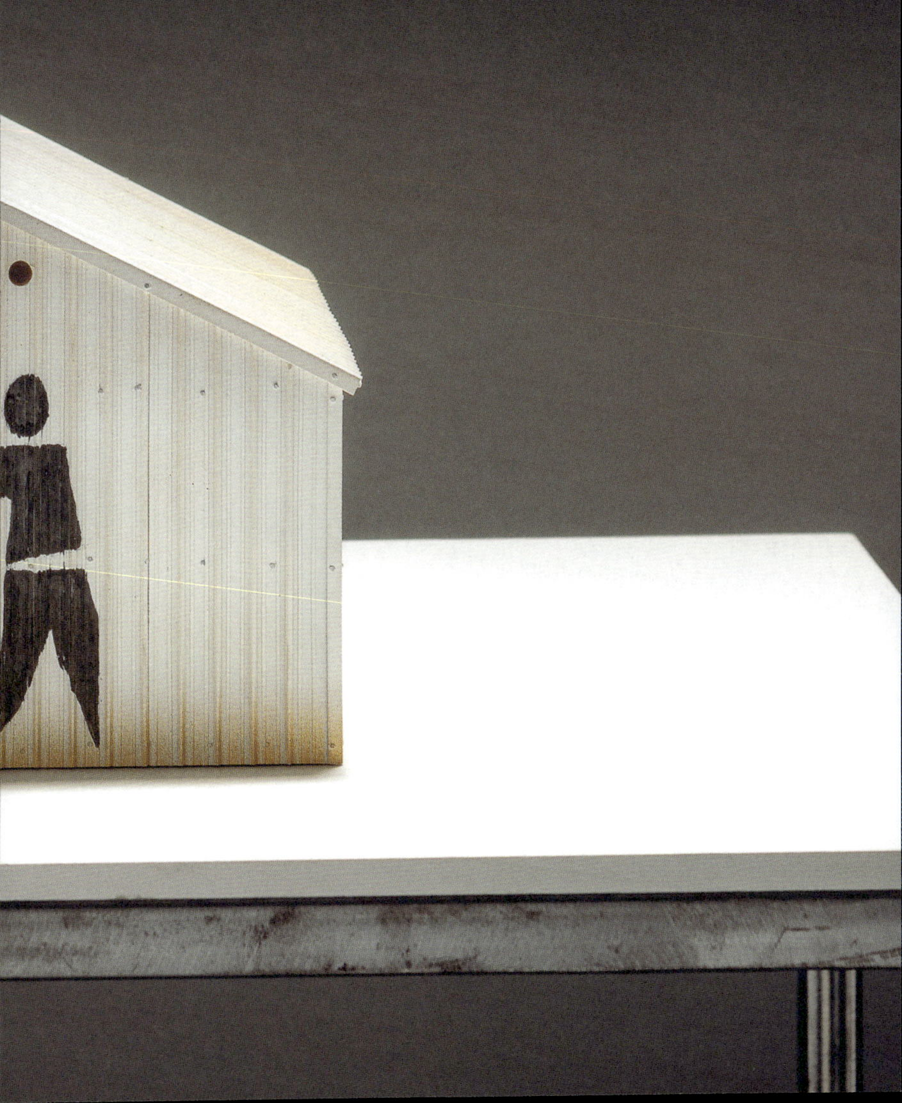

*Azraq*, 2016

# Azraq

## *Annemarie Jacir*

dream blue
azraq azure
wake up to zinc
dream embrace
love
        zinc zinc
dream
zinc roof zinc walls
summer like a blaze winter like death
here your row
here your number
here home new shiny modern
        no electricity
here where your mother will die
after a life of bread   earth   village

at 4 o'clock in the morning the jinn
dream floats upwards
                                        disintegrate
break apart like waves, gentle
no trace

bodies are pulled from the Nile
bodies from the Seine
our Tigris our Euphrates
again and again we lose
                                        home

here where you will die
after a life of bread earth
                    green and azure

here. until we say
                                        go

# Interactive Fiction :: Windows

## *Hala Alyan*

Every time I tell the story I warp it. The song is playing in another car and I call

*Fatima*

but it's my own pocket
that buzzes, my chest
rising to steal her

dialect. We're back on
the balcony. The balcony
is beneath

water. The water is
violet with trash. I curl
against her in bed—

Pillow, grandmother.
The things you endured:
Vienna, beehive hair,

the magazines we left in
a pile by your door, with
their tropical islands and

mascara. Salim and his
sons. A house you hated.
The only one you had.

*Nadia*

and we talk about hair and
Damascus, our bad luck
with men. I like to debate
fortunes, and she tells me

to pack God like a ribbon in
my tote bag. She's alive in
the coral tree, cursing the
traffic and Americans. She

waited for me after all, in
that restaurant by the sea
where the waiters sang to
each other and we both

wore yellow and I told her
how Paris made me want to
start my life over. Where
we have lives to start over.

*nobody*

and I've been in the
bath for an hour,

listening to the
voicemails and peeling

callouses from my
palm. I ask what I

never asked. I pray in
the direction of them.

Years ago, I got naked
in an Istanbul hammam

and as the woman
scrubbed me, I said

*they love me like a*
*crime already forgiven.*

When someone dies, their love converts into

*a house*

with a single rotting
chair     I talk to the
moon about family and

salvation          I talk to
the moon like it's God
I don't have one middle

name       I have six and
not a single one of them
my mother

I want to sleep
          in that house
plummy with death

but I bloom          instead
orchid          dance with
my uncle in the heat of a

club          all our words
spent          the music
splits into a          moon

*your voice*

reciting three anthems. The
one that repeats, the one

that interrupts, and the one
that ends. I'm west of

their graves. The acacia
trees. The bed to dance

a river into. It was leaving
that made me American,

not the other way around.
This is why we stopped

drinking. This is why every
door has a circle of blue

glass to ward off the evil
eye. But what of my eyes,

my envy, my take. Nadia
tells me to open the curtain

*water*

on the meditation tape,
in the nightstand glass,
all around my plunged
ears. Every ocean is

another ocean, one that
died inside it and left its
bones. I darken myself
with sun and language.

Nadia, I'll name her
Nadia. I'll tell her Syria
has waited long enough.
I'll draw the ace of

cups from the card deck
and cry. On the other
side of the world, God's
house begins to burn

and I dress myself by that light.

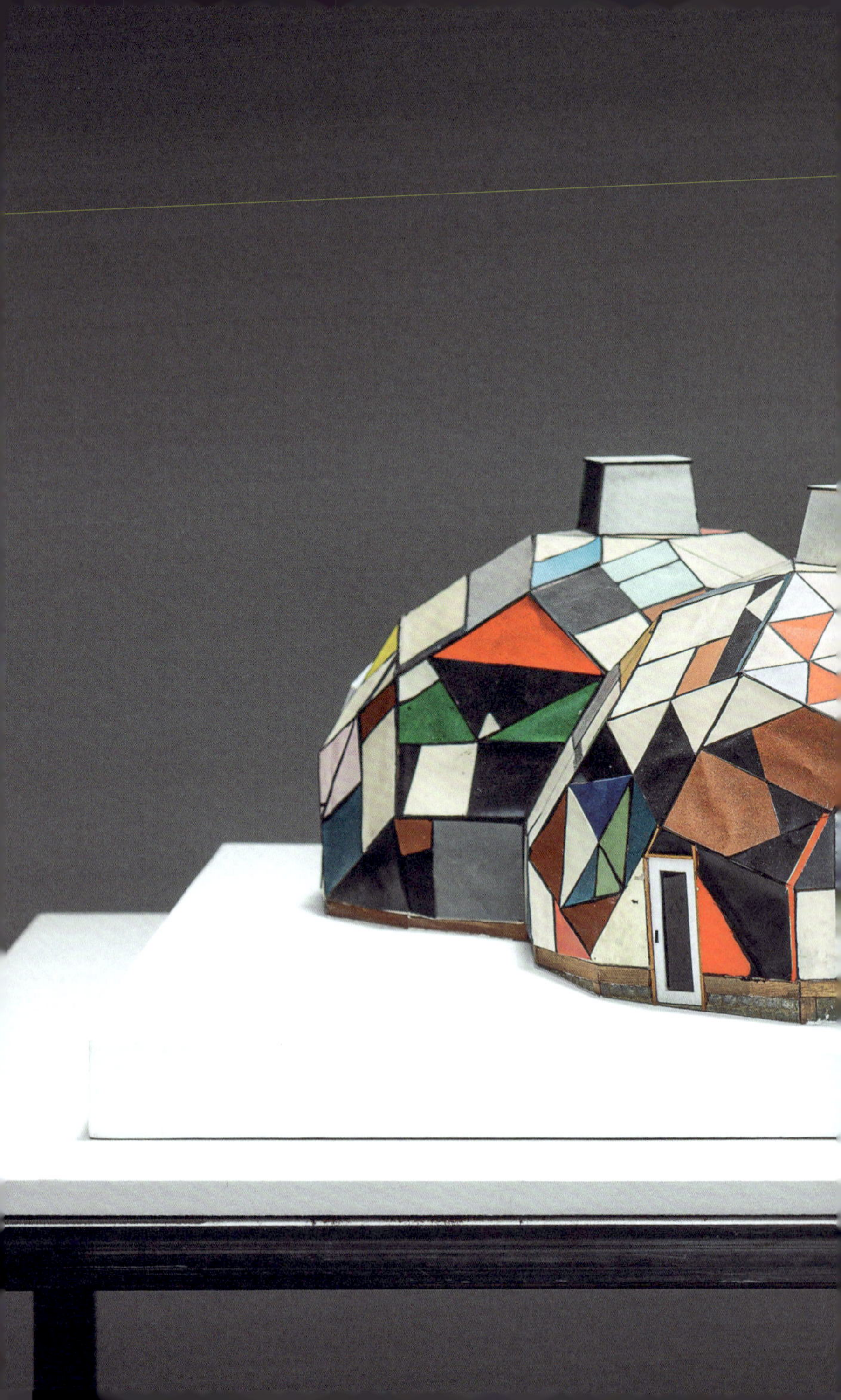

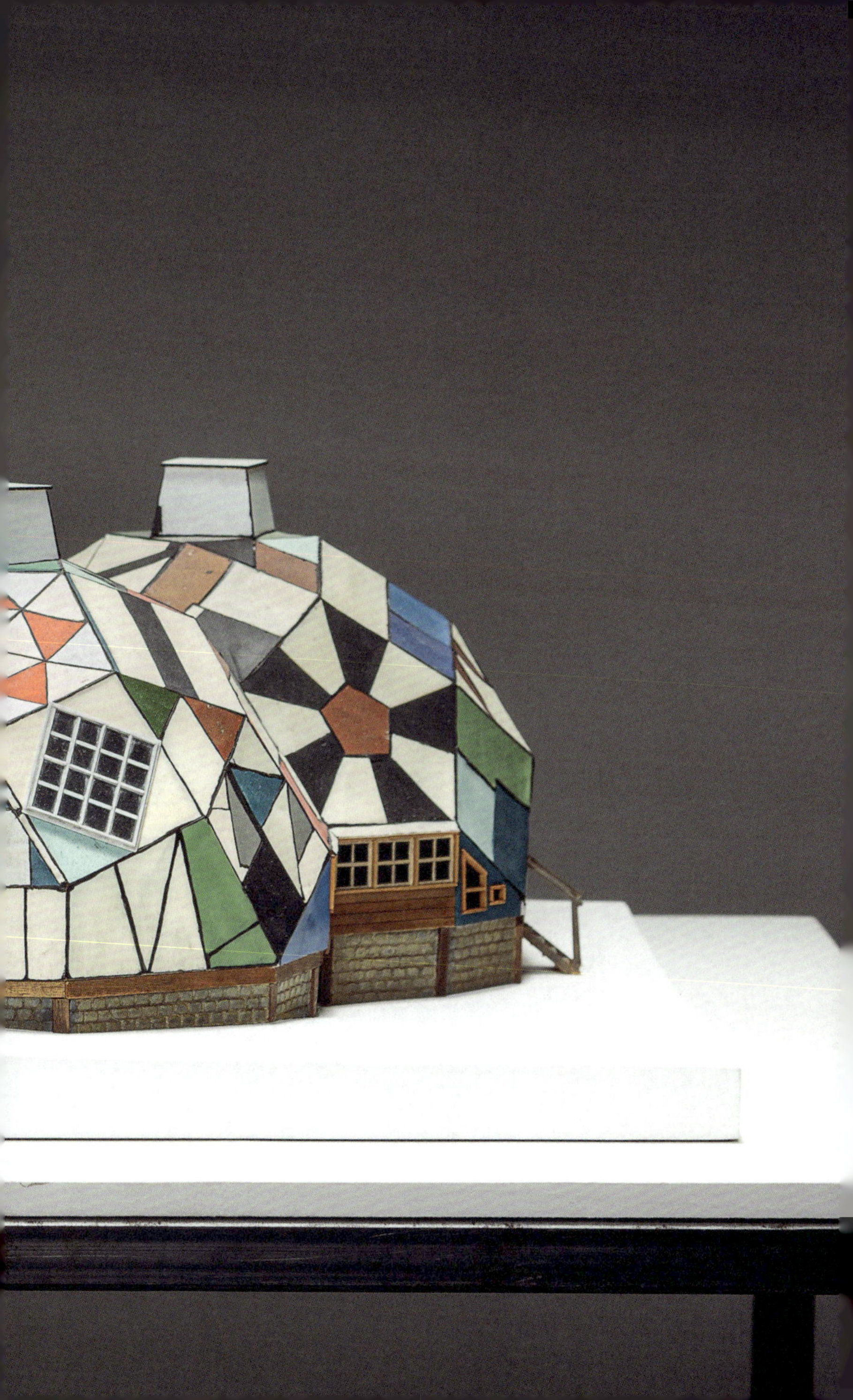

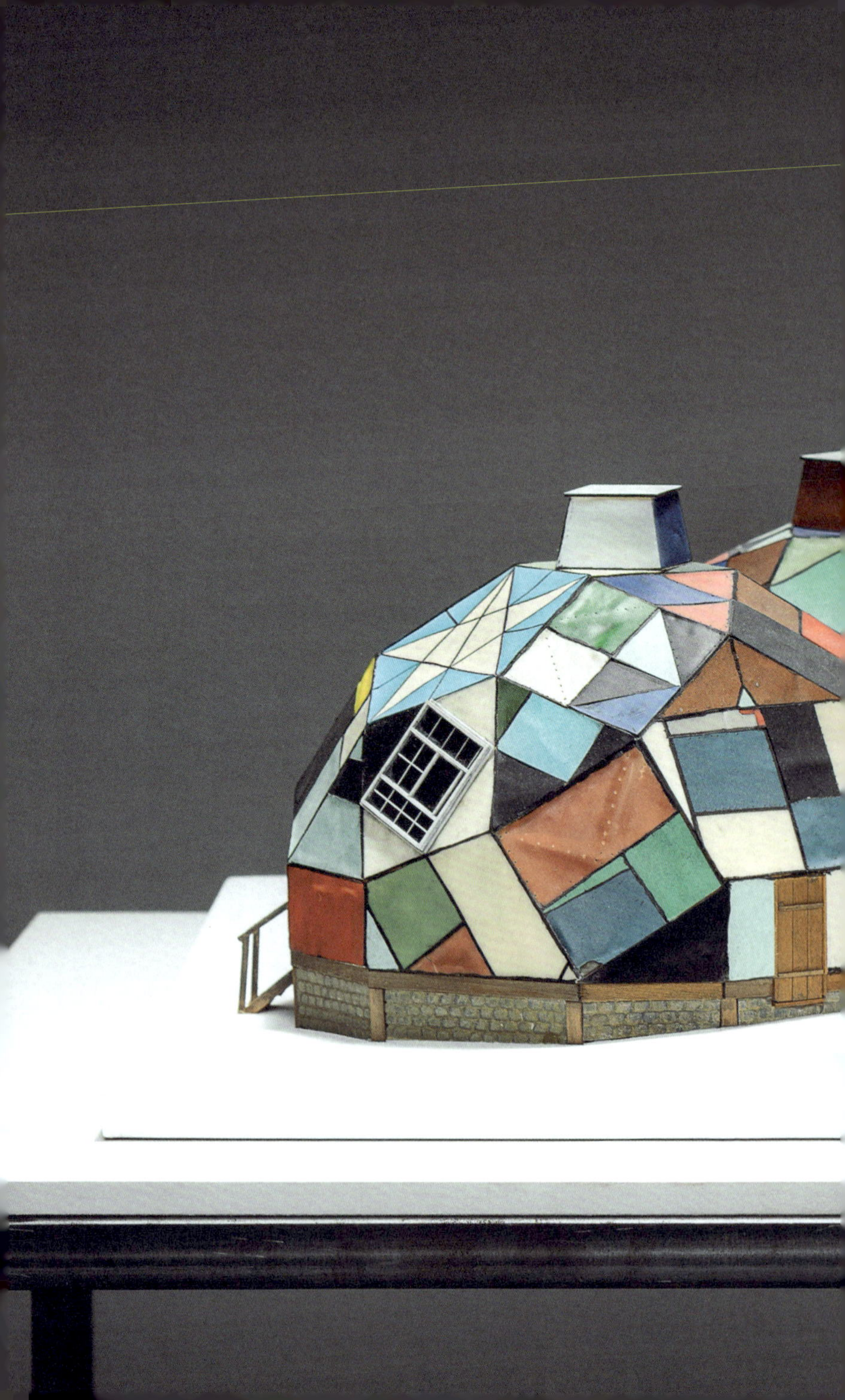

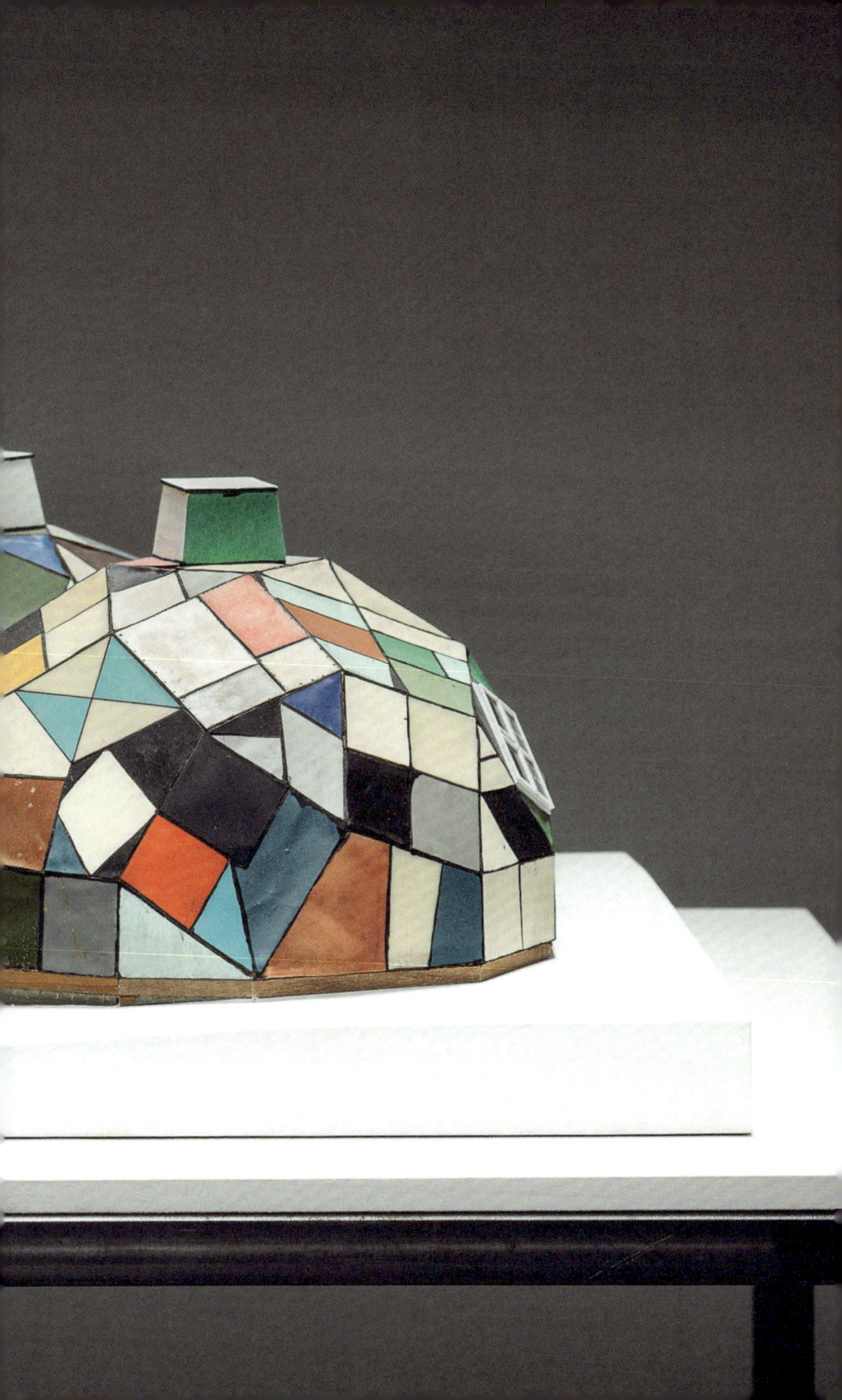

*Dome*, 2016

# Untitled (Euclidean)

## *Renee Gladman*

*If magnitude, taken separately, be proportionals,* be shapes of light, be events dividing along the lines of inside and outside, and faces turning to and away from light, the round of the ceiling being the frame for looking back at the day, and you've divided your day into the left and right rounds of the dome structure and have thought in one and fucked in the other and are now sitting along the line between, looking up at the sheltered day, you being sheltered: we. And somebody lets sounds enter from the street—we're trying to build something whole but intricate—and the voices be proportional to the throats from which they're emitted (she's trying to find the black voices); and the door closes and makes another line and gives another opportunity to stand, to fuck, to think, to study the partitions of light that block the sky, your blue, your magenta, like we're all living according to the spectrum: these will be your events. But every time the door opens the dome shifts; more people enter. Voices take the interior of the space and turn the whole thing into volume; they bring in stories from outside, make the shape you're living radial "Are you picking up what we're putting down?" gets left, a gift to the form, while the constant of bodies squeezing into the interior (time separating from the structure) becomes a throng. This is dome living:

people be proportionals to your thinking, to your wondering where she is within the throng and wondering about the portions of light discernible to the eye—are they in any kind of order? And she'll be in the part of the dome you can't feel from within the dome: somebody comes and tells you. Look up, be proportional to the wall expanding and the third round of the dome, be the magnitude of the first and second round, be where the line empties out, be the third round that holds the books and protects the books from light; we be dark in the third round, reading under soft light, and taken separately, each in our own study, swept up in the histories of things, how many times—and the voices work against the skin, make you want people to draw closer, make you want some unified living. To think within some magnitude of a black voice unfolding, and running through every other possible voice, so that there is always something breaking something ready and something moving to something stilled and a third shape growing from the memories of other voices, and this is where the light is most intense. You in your orange, your brown.

# Pocket Universe

## *Nalo Hopkinson*

Sadika grimaced as the artist case-worker fitted the visor over her head. They'd swabbed the rubber seal with alcohol after the last person used it, but the alcohol was still wet and warm as sweat. It had soaked into the worn rubber. The visor sealed against her face with a squelch.

"Comfy?" the artist asked. Alistair, he said his name was. Trim, ageless black man, managed to make his hospital whites and matching tennis shoes look dapper. His voice came conducted through the bones in her ears, eerily both intimate and distant. He didn't wait for Sadika to reply. "Okay; sight, smell, touch, hearing, or taste?"

Sadika relaxed gingerly against the couch's cushions, wincing against anticipated pain. Painkillers hadn't quite kicked in yet. Doctors said the soreness in her back was because her lungs were now affected. "Affected." Such a neutral word for what was really going on in her body.

But the movement hurt less than she'd expected. The couch cradled her without compressing any part of her. "Just bury me in this then, nuh?" she joked. "I feel like I lying in angel wings and cotton puffs."

Alistair chuckled. "Be amazed how many patients ask that. All right. Pick one of your five senses, please."

Sadika sighed, the movement of her inhalation bringing

a dull echo of an internal elbow to the ribs. She considered for a few seconds. "Taste."

She'd thought she would feel something from the sensors all over her scalp, suckered onto her poor bald scalp like leeches. Instead, her mouth sprang water as it filled with the starchy, liquid pleasure that was Maami's red peas soup. "Mi lawd!" she exclaimed, and automatically held her hands to her mouth to catch the liquid she was sure would spill from it. But of course there was nothing there.

Alistair's amused voice in her ear said, "Don't worry. No food not really in your mouth."

But it might as well have been. Sadika let the soup taste dance over her tongue. Salty, like her grandmother had liked it. Maami's pressure was what had killed her, but she'd always eaten just what she wanted. Said life was too short deny herself.

But the sensation in her mouth was too cold, though, and too slimy. Sadika wasn't sure what her brain did to communicate that to the interface, but in a few seconds, it was just right. Warm and something else. Unguent; that was the word. Then the conviction she was tasting soup faded entirely.

Alistair said, "Sorry about that. I had the gain up too high, and you got some feedback. But I can use what I got. Pick another sensation, please, Miss Lawton."

"I could pick taste again? Or it have to be something else?"

"Up to you. You don't have to do anything in order. Is your resting place, after all. You just tell me what you want."

"That's the problem. I don't know what I want."

"Tell me what you're most proud of in your life."

"Who, me? What somebody like me have to be proud of, or not be proud of? I get born, I lived, and now I dying.

When I gone, my ashes going to rest in the burial house you making me. So just make me a house then, nuh?"

"Yes, but the house have to come from you. It have to sum up your life, come from your imagination. Try touch. What memories you get from that?"

Sadika focused on the bulbs of her fingertips, on what they made her think of. "I guess I'm supposed to be thinking about the feel of my babies' skins soft under my hands, or of a lover."

Alistair smiled, his features lit by the glow from the monitor. "If you want. Though in my line of work, we call that a cliché."

Sadika chuckled. "I see." In any case, the sensation making her fingers tingle wasn't the expected. It was a smooth, metallic, moveable. And a pulling feeling that went a little way up her arm, accompanied by a click.

"What is that?" Alistair asked.

"Car doors. The handles."

"Huh. Different cars?"

"Yeah. Passenger sides, mostly. I used to work the stroll, you know. When I was young. The one down on the east side. I got into plenty plenty cars."

"Me, too," Alistair replied. "Started there as a poor young artist. I didn't like all those different people touching me all the time, but some of them were nice. I decided I liked the comfort work business, so now I do this." He fiddled with his screen. Its back was to her.

Sadika grunted. "I never thought too much about liking it or hating it. It was a job. I was good at it, is all."

"So why you want to make it part of your coffin memorial?"

Sadika let the sense-memory from her fingertips extend all the way through her body. The cramped spaces in all those cars, the tiny universe each one had created, stretched to bursting to hold two people for a short space of time. The sliding of slick, damp flesh against and in hers. The comforting smell of warm skin and latex. The muscle-fatigued ache in her jaw and her nethers after a busy night. The shudders and moans she elicited. Not always quiet. No two people came exactly the same way. She'd never lost interest in that. She was proud of the work she'd done.

She began to try to put it all into words for Alistair, but he shook his head and smiled. "Just think about it all," he said. "The sensors can tell which centers of your brain are lighting up."

He busied himself for a few minutes. "What else you want me to add in?" he asked.

The little bit of effort she'd expended on this had exhausted her. Irritably, she snapped, "Don't you have enough already?"

His reply was mild. "I do. Lie there and rest while the maquette rendering."

Now she felt bad for taking it out on him. Trying to make up for it, she said, "But you have people waiting, don't it?"

"Don't worry out your soul case. You rest little bit."

Alistair traced on the touch screen of his laptop, made mysterious gestures in the air. Sadika kind of wished she could see what he was doing, but he'd show it to her soon enough. Her mind drifted. She drifted a lot nowadays. All those powerful painkillers.

After more minutes than she'd kept track of, Alistair murmured. "Keep your eyes closed, Miss Sadika. I going to unhook you from this contraption. Then open your eyes slowly."

She didn't. She wanted to see what her memory had

made. But her eyes opened onto darkness. Alistair had turned off the lights. She savored the dark, enclosed space. Just the two of them. For a short time longer.

Alistair said, "I going to on the light slow. Take time to get used to it."

"Chuh, man." Sadika didn't have time. Days, maybe. Weeks if she was lucky. Or unlucky. Truth to tell, Sadika was tired, to rass. Tired to her bones. This sickness wasted muscle, stole breath, made you a baby again. She struggled to sit up, clenched her teeth so as not to complain about Alistair's gentle hands helping her up. He plumped pillows behind her back while she strained to see the form on the screen he had turned towards her.

Smooth and bumpy. Round like bowls full of red peas soup, but made up of angles, all kinda different angles. Plenty plenty colours. Shaped by all those car doors into two joined domes, fat like bubbies, and, like hers, two slightly different sizes. The cancer had started in her left one. It pleased Sadika to think that her dead house would call her breasts to mind, for those who had eyes to see. Those breasts had fed her babies, had been suckled on by eager johns and lovers. Had given her and others pleasure.

She straightened up little more, to better see the maquette. No, it had three lobes, not two. Three, two; didn't matter. She used to have two breasts. Now she had one whole one and two scarred bumps, the keloided remainders of the other one. And pretty soon, she would be dust, and would have no bubbies at all.

"No handles on the doors?" she asked Alistair.

"You didn't imagine handles."

"Probably because I won't be getting out these doors."

He nodded. "A-true. You like it?"

"How big it going to be?"

"Big enough to hold your ashes. I think I will get car doors from the junk yard. Cut them in pieces. Weld them into the shape you see here."

"How long?"

"Maybe a week. You think you can hang on that long?"

She laughed. It hurt. "I will try. If not, them can just put me on ice till my new house ready for me."

She contemplated the rendering again. "I like it." She took the artist's hand, pressed it to her bosom. Her "affected" bosom. "Thank you."

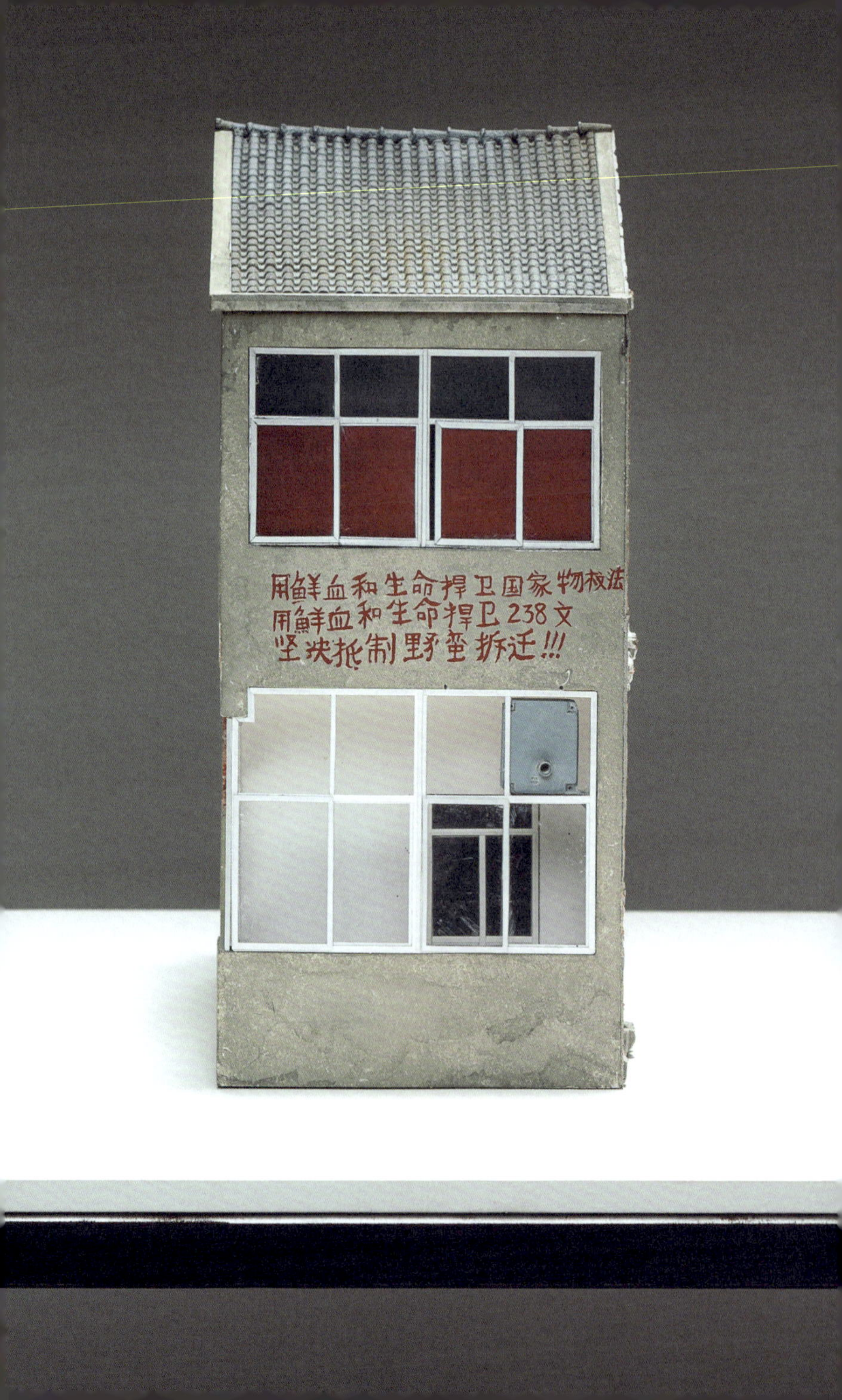
用鲜血和生命捍卫国家物校法
用鲜血和生命捍卫238文
坚决抵制野蛮拆迁!!!

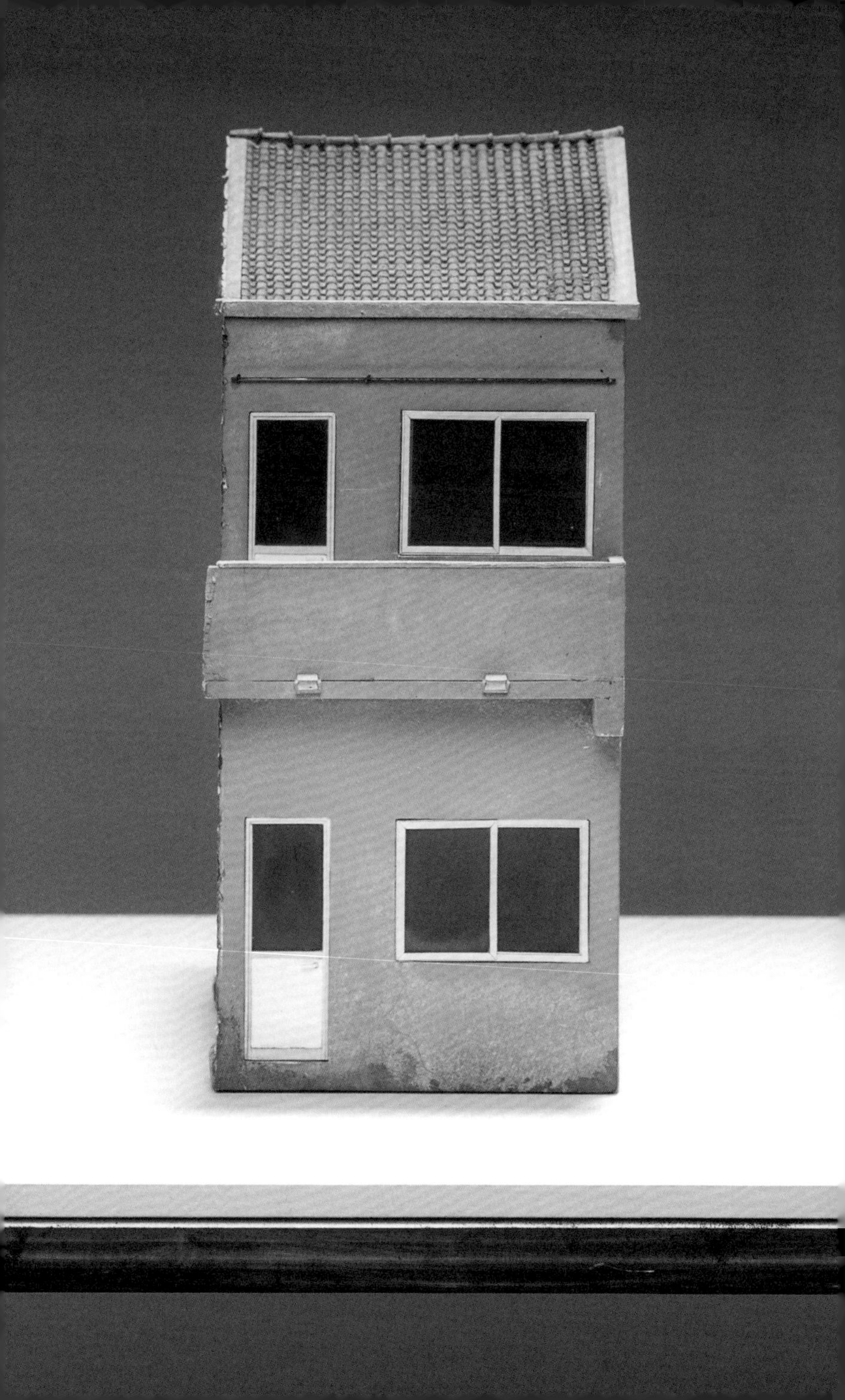

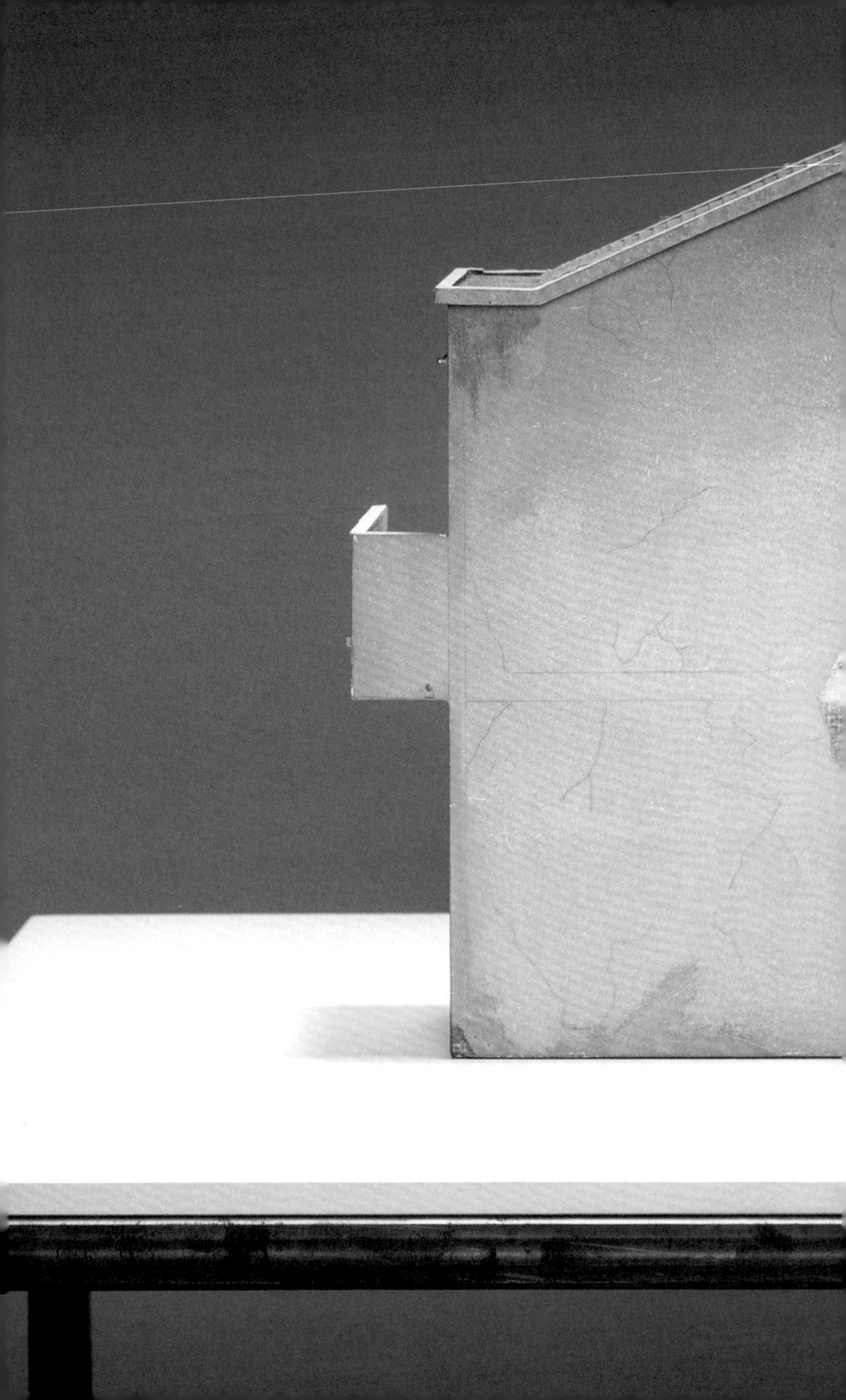

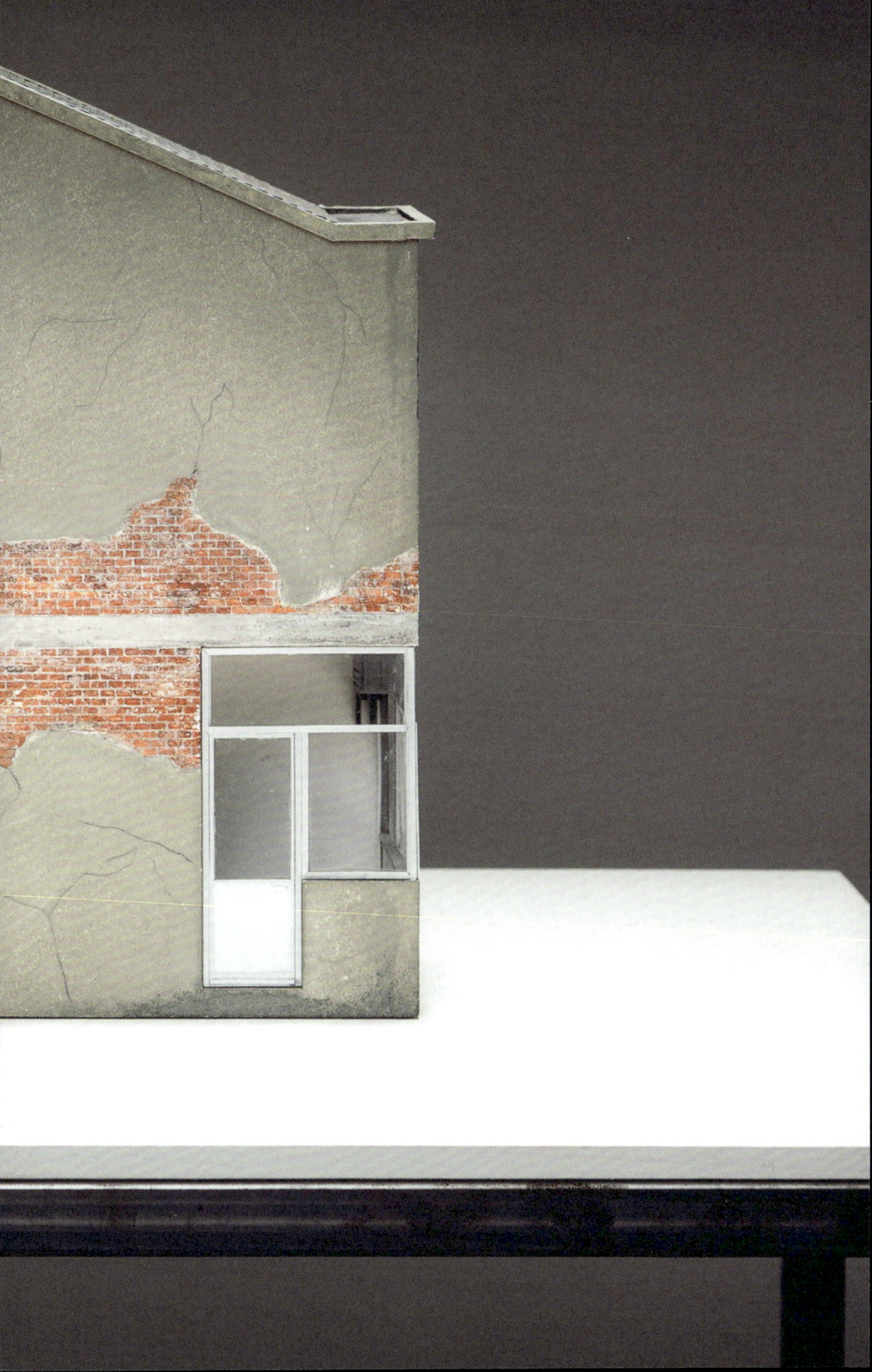

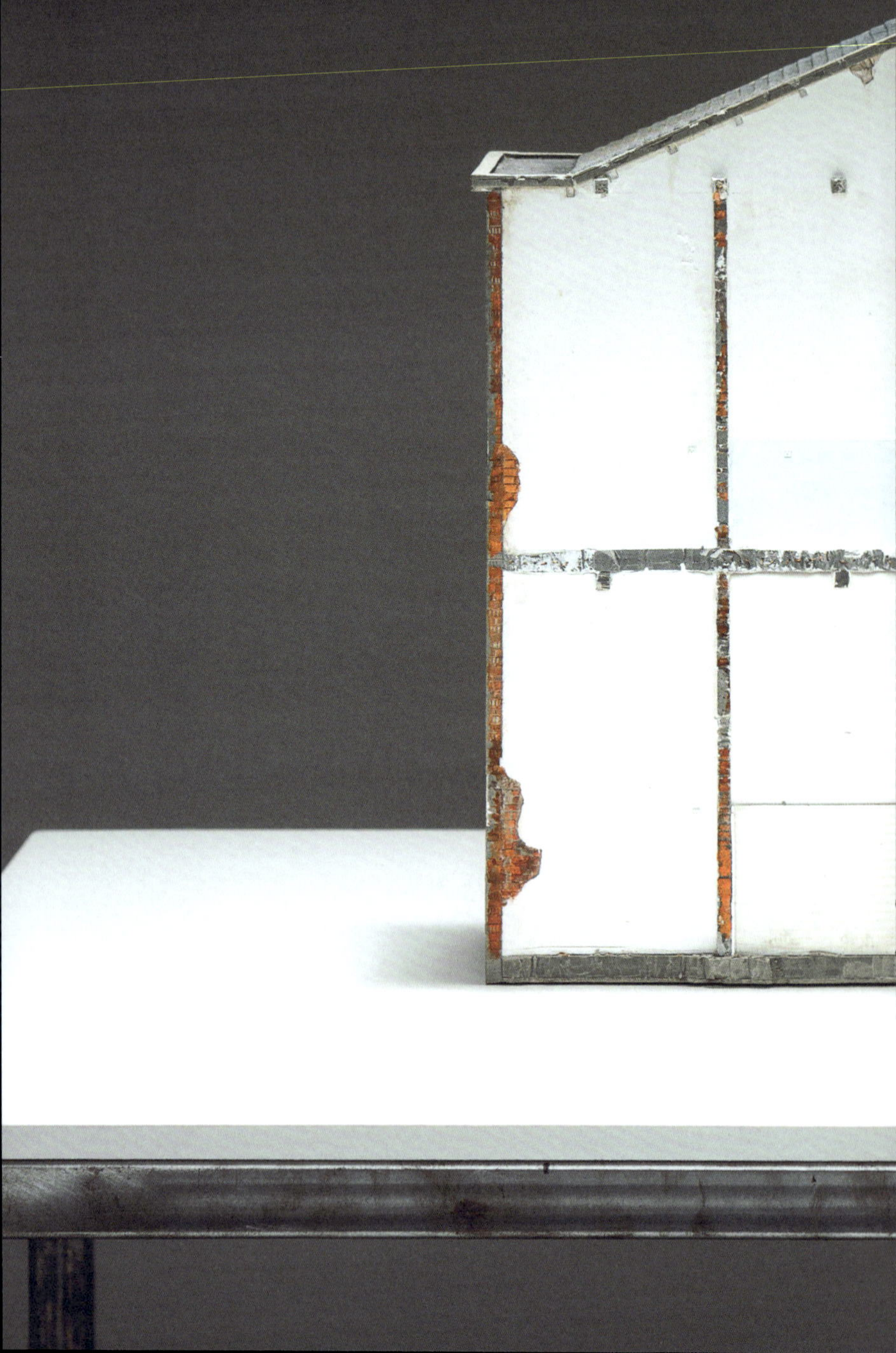

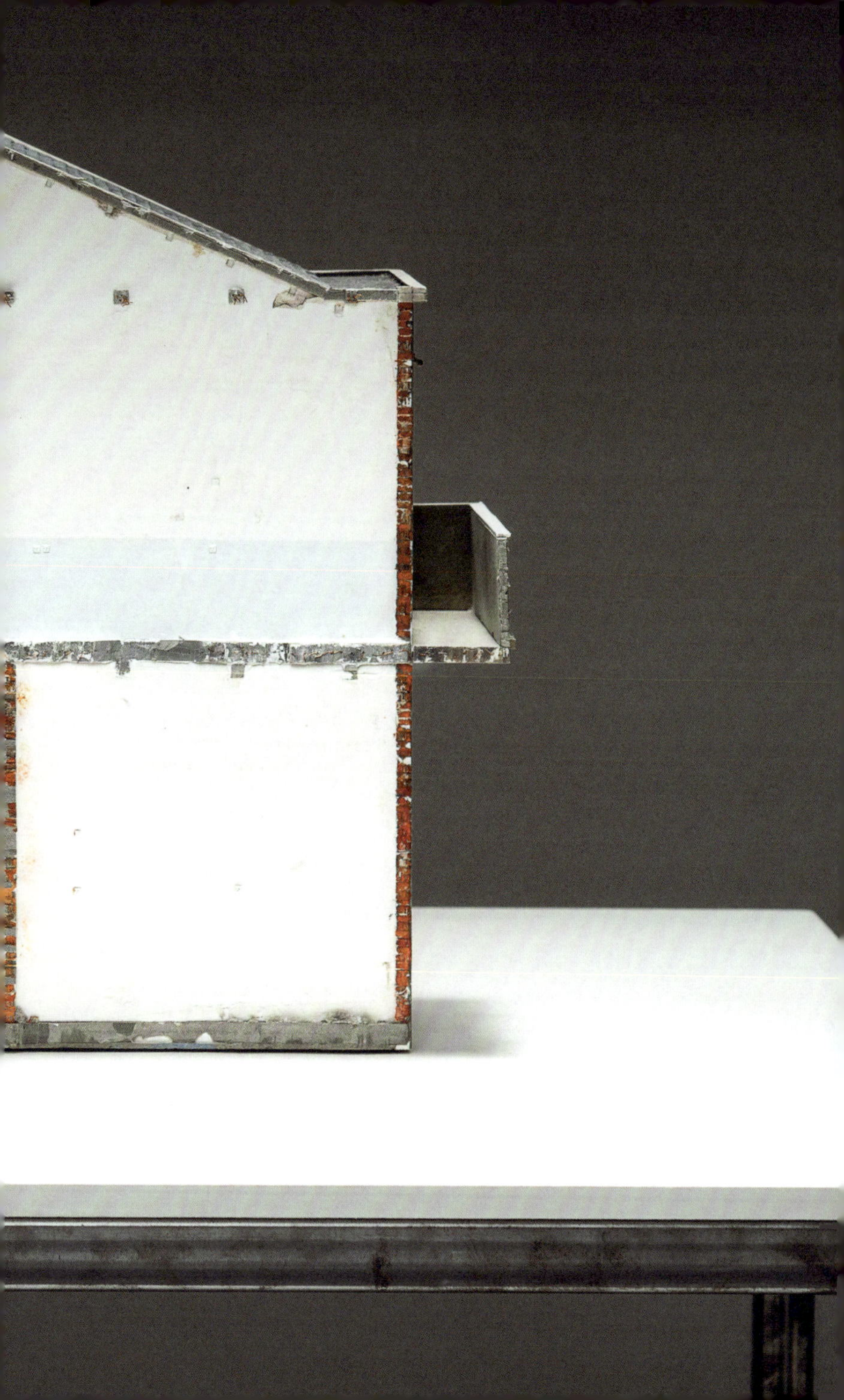

*Holdout*, 2016

# Holdout 198

# *Madeleine Thien*

Many years after my mother died, I went to visit her in the apartment where I had grown up. We sat on the sofa and my mother told me that, all her life, she had disliked the furniture in this little room. But, she said, since passing on, her feelings for the desk, the bed and the faded, rosewood tables had changed. "Against my better judgment," she said, "I find these pieces beautiful now."

She was wearing a mauve dress that fell to her knees in narrow pleats, her hair was curled, and when she smiled, she looked intense and beautiful. She looked younger than the last time I had seen her, more than a decade ago.

"Are you in a hurry to get back?" she asked. "You could stay for lunch."

"I would like that."

I heard the stutter of a car starting, a door slamming, the hum of a refrigerator. In the distance, rooftops were crowned with satellite dishes and thin, silvery antennae.

"Your sister went to buy coffee," my mother said. "She should be back any minute."

I nodded. Everything in my mother's apartment—a room that no longer exists (when she died, all the furniture was given away. I had taken her files and papers to the city's recycling depot, where a worker had instructed me to upend them into a machine that compacted and shredded them, so that even her handwriting had disappeared. The apartment was given up)—was achingly familiar.

The traffic on this little street grew heavier, grew slower. Birds appeared, moving from window to window, then vanishing. My mother said I needed more sleep, she said my hair was too long, I should wear warmer clothes, eat more meat, read less in bed. I asked her if she was happy and she smiled and said, "Oh, well, of course I'm happy." I wanted to tell her all the stories I had saved up, the things that had changed in my life, but it didn't seem the time.

No one came to the door and no coffee arrived and my mother no longer seemed to expect anyone. Afternoon dissolved into evening and we sat together in contemplative silence. I was hungry but no food appeared, and I understood that if I went outside the room, if I tried to find the kitchen, I might be disappointed. I could not remember how I had come here, whether through the window or door, or some other means. I did not know how this room attached to all the others through which I had passed, all my life, whether they were joined like the ribs of a skeleton or whether they floated in space, and it was only by chance that we had both passed this way again.

I hoped my mother would tell me about her existence but, as in life, she did not wish to talk about herself. Instead she laughed at my jokes and looked into my eyes as I tried to make light of our situation. The things we left unspoken grew high around us, solidifying like a gate or a wall, sheltering the objects I could not let go of, this dress, this room, the familiar and the beloved.

"Go on," she said kindly. "It's long past dinner time and you haven't eaten all day."

Before I left, she gave me a stack of clothes, and I accepted them in order to please her even though I did not need more socks or sweaters or skirts. Neither did she, of course. She said I had not let her down. Or, at least, these were the words I heard when she let go of my hand.

On my return the following day, I had difficulty finding the apartment. The air was filled with dust. When at last I located the door, I saw that half the building had been cut away.

Inside, thankfully, nothing had changed and no rooms had been dislodged. My mother was seated at the table, which was piled high with what appeared to be bills or even taxes. I went to the window. The distant rooftops with their silvery antennae were no longer visible. I berated myself for having struggled to find the apartment when hardly any other buildings stood.

My mother pushed aside the calculator. "Six months," she said. "It was the longest I could get." She gave a small shrug. "They couldn't spare me."

I was happy and also heavy, as if I were descending slowly through the air. Six months from now, it would be summer. My mother's hands were soft, like something newly made.

We watched television just as we used to do, and eventually my mother fell asleep on the sofa. Her mug of warm water cooled. I watched the slowness of her breathing and later I watched her dream, and I fell asleep to a dream of her dreaming. When next I opened my eyes, morning light was inching across the room. I went out and saw that the entire street had disappeared, except for a single flip flop, a taxi receipt, a broken suitcase, and a heap of blue roof tiles waiting to be salvaged. Beyond the street, nothing.

In order to make things last, we ate very little. We sorted

her clothes and set aside things that might, one day, be donated and reused. She did Tai Chi every morning, and I would pretend not to be looking from the window as the dust moved around her, sometimes obscuring her. It was like watching a painting slowly being painted, or a portrait revised. One morning city planners appeared. Construction workers arrived by bus. I began to see beams of light sliding across the night sky, as if the workers never slept. I had a sharpened sense of myself and my mother. I saw that I had not helped her as much as I might have. And yet, even when I had disappointed her, she had remained constant. In life, she had often relented to others. But relented how, I now wondered. And wasn't the right word *acquiesced?* I had trouble understanding things.

The fourth month came and went. She tried to negotiate for more time but her letters came back unopened. The television ceased to work, and one day disappeared. "It can't be helped," my mother said. We began to sneak out of the house at dawn and twilight, always unsure if we should. Sometimes we walked through the new neighborhood, whose houses glimmered like waves in the sun. We pointed out new items on display in the shops. We admired the hanging gardens and balustrades, the unexpected appearance of a river, the newness of traffic jams.

"I grew up beside the sea, did I ever tell you?" she said one night as an orange glow slipped under the horizon.

"In Kowloon?"

She nodded. "For weeks, while we watched, workers pumped out the water. One day, the harbor was gone, replaced by concrete. Our street was renamed Reclamation Street to mark the place where the South China Sea had been."

"I didn't know."

"You could still smell the water," she said. "All of your senses said it was there, except your eyes."

The fifth month lasted a lifetime. I could no longer find the sofa. I slept beside her in the bed. She seemed frailer to me.

"I was born in China," she said one night.

I answered sleepily, "No, you always said you'd never been to China."

"Yes," she said. "I never went, but I was born there. In sixty thousand years, maybe you're the first in our family not to be born there." And then, after a moment, "Your sister went to buy coffee."

I was glad the darkness prevented her from seeing me. "She should be back any minute," I said.

I thought my mother had fallen asleep, but then she said, "What does life feel like now?"

I had no answer. It was so quiet around us.

Our building was supposed to come down years ago. There were people living upstairs, an octogenarian couple who seemed to have no children. Except for a door shutting, or the occasional murmur of a television, I rarely heard them. I read about them on my phone. They had been nicknamed the "bullet-headed couple" and I could see why. When this street was marked for development, one thousand households were evicted and the buildings torn down. But the bullet-headed ones had refused to go. The surrounding ground was excavated and they were left high in the air, as if balanced atop a finger. "These stubborn homeowners are like a rusty nail!" people exclaimed. Refusing to come free.

The elderly woman corrected them. "We're like a small

boat, she said, in the middle of the ocean."

Her husband clarified, "We'll stay until the end of the world."

The plot they owned was just a tiny square. Eventually, years later, the excavated land around them was filled in once more.

When the sixth month came, I unearthed my mother's dictionary, looking for a way to say goodbye but it was difficult. The pages were fading and growing thinner. I discovered that *bài,* a loan word, combines "hand" 手 and "the sound of the waves, turbulence" 湃 to create the word *bài* 拜 or 拜 拜 *bye bye!* A club had opened next door and late into the night people gathered and danced, they emerged looped together like strings of pearls, glimmering down the promenade along the brand new river. For an entire week, people hunted the Pokémon trapped against our front window. One morning, I found there were no windows at all, only frames. I covered the space with paper. Bit by bit, more things had to be replaced. I was concerned about the walls. When I ran my hand against them, they made a rustling noise, like a creature in retreat.

Reclining on the sofa, using her housecoat as a blanket, my mother said, "These days a paper map is outdated by the time you print it."

"When you died," I said, "someone stole the books from your bedroom. And your opera binoculars."

"I know who did it. They came to my funeral with empty suitcases but when they left, their suitcases were full."

We laughed because it was true.

Nighttime gradually filled the room.

My mother said, "I meant to tidy everything up for you but here we are, already six months gone."

"Don't worry, I'll take care of everything."

"It's summer now, isn't it?"

I nodded. I thought I could hear something from the next room, cicadas, a humming. I realized too late that I was no longer able to see her, even though I could hear her voice as clearly as before.

"The elderly couple upstairs," she said. "It's true. They'll stay until the end of the world."

"I hope so."

"When I'm gone, tell them to move down here. The stairs are difficult for them."

"I will." I asked her if she remembered that when I published my first book, she had put her copy under one leg of the dining table, to keep the table steady.

"It was the right thickness," she said, and smiled in apology and love. "It's still there."

Six months could also be a lifetime, I told myself.

"Dress warmer," my mother told me one last time.

I nodded and she kissed me goodbye.

Afterwards, I went upstairs and told the couple she was gone. From up there, I could see the turning of the river, how it looped back on itself and seemed to slide over its own body, how it ran underneath the soil, as if we were standing in it now without knowing.

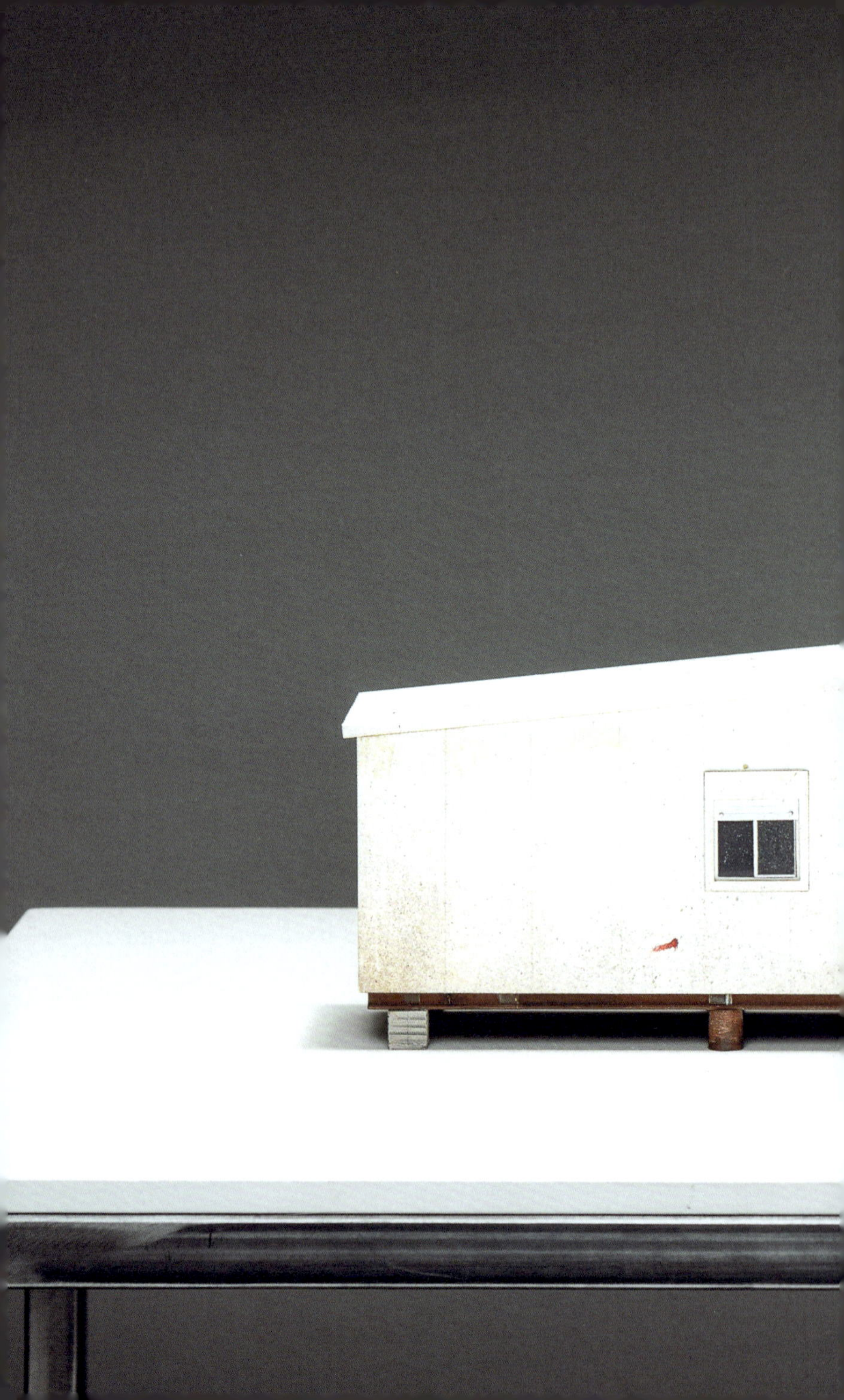

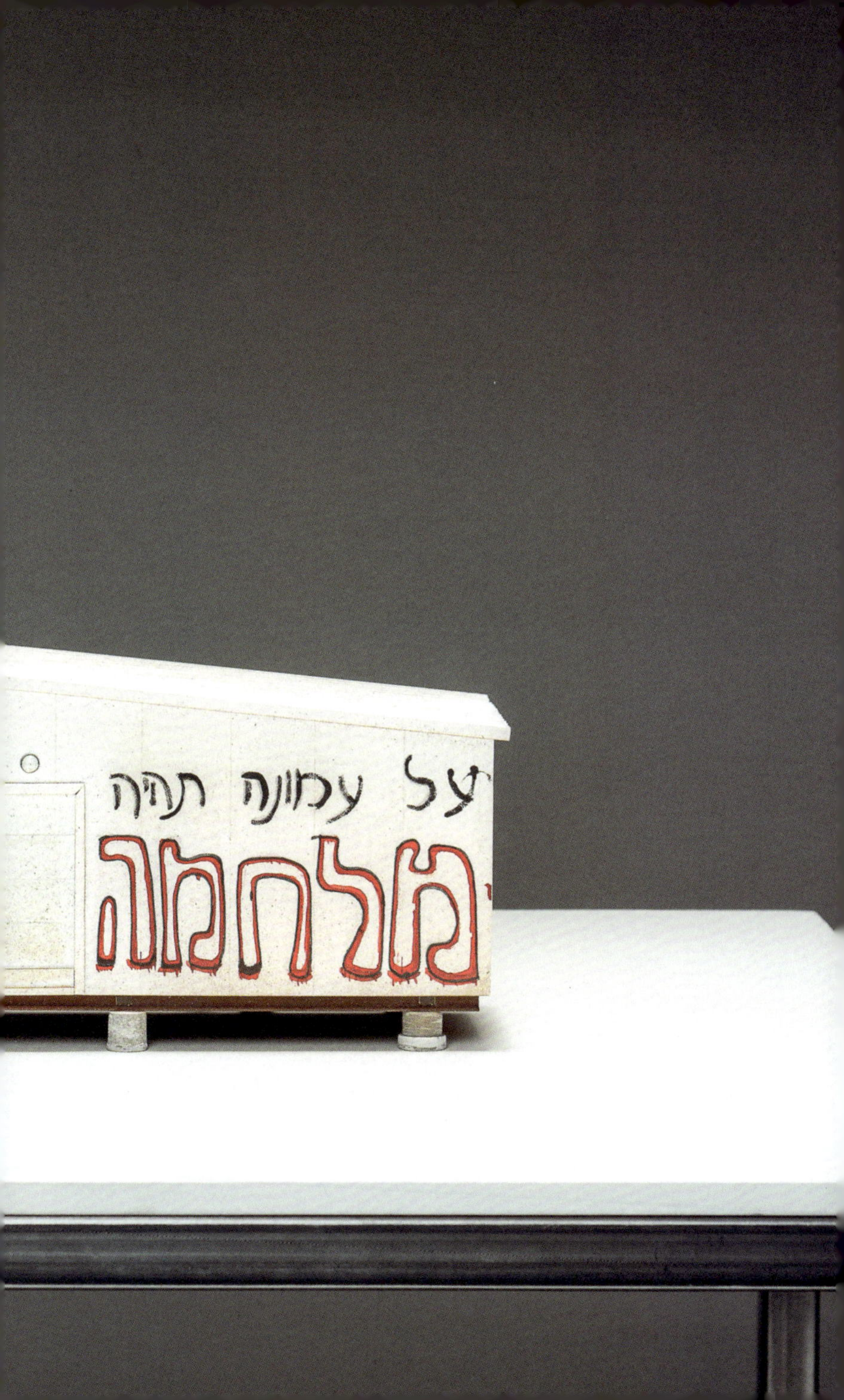
על עמונה תהיה
מלחמה

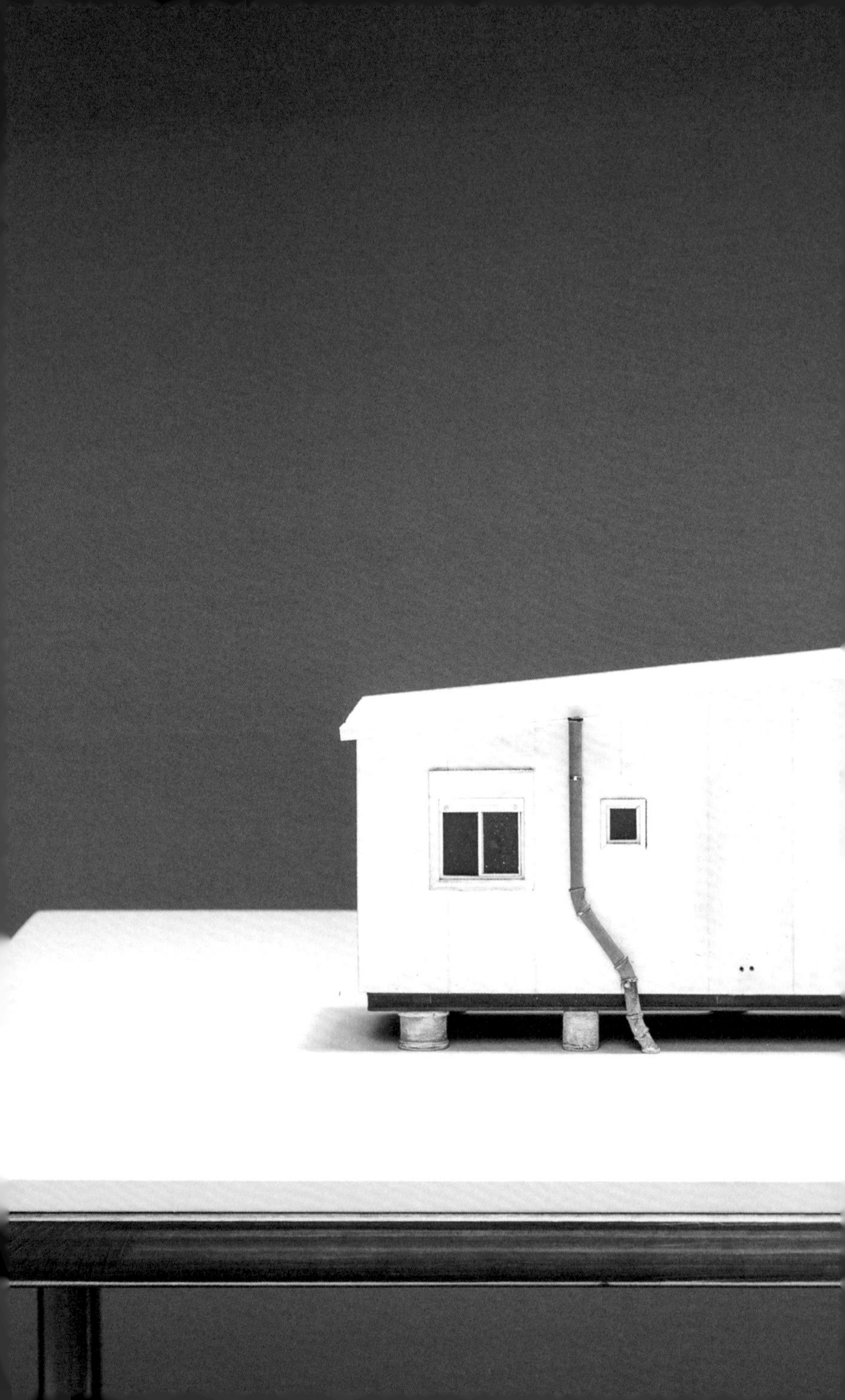

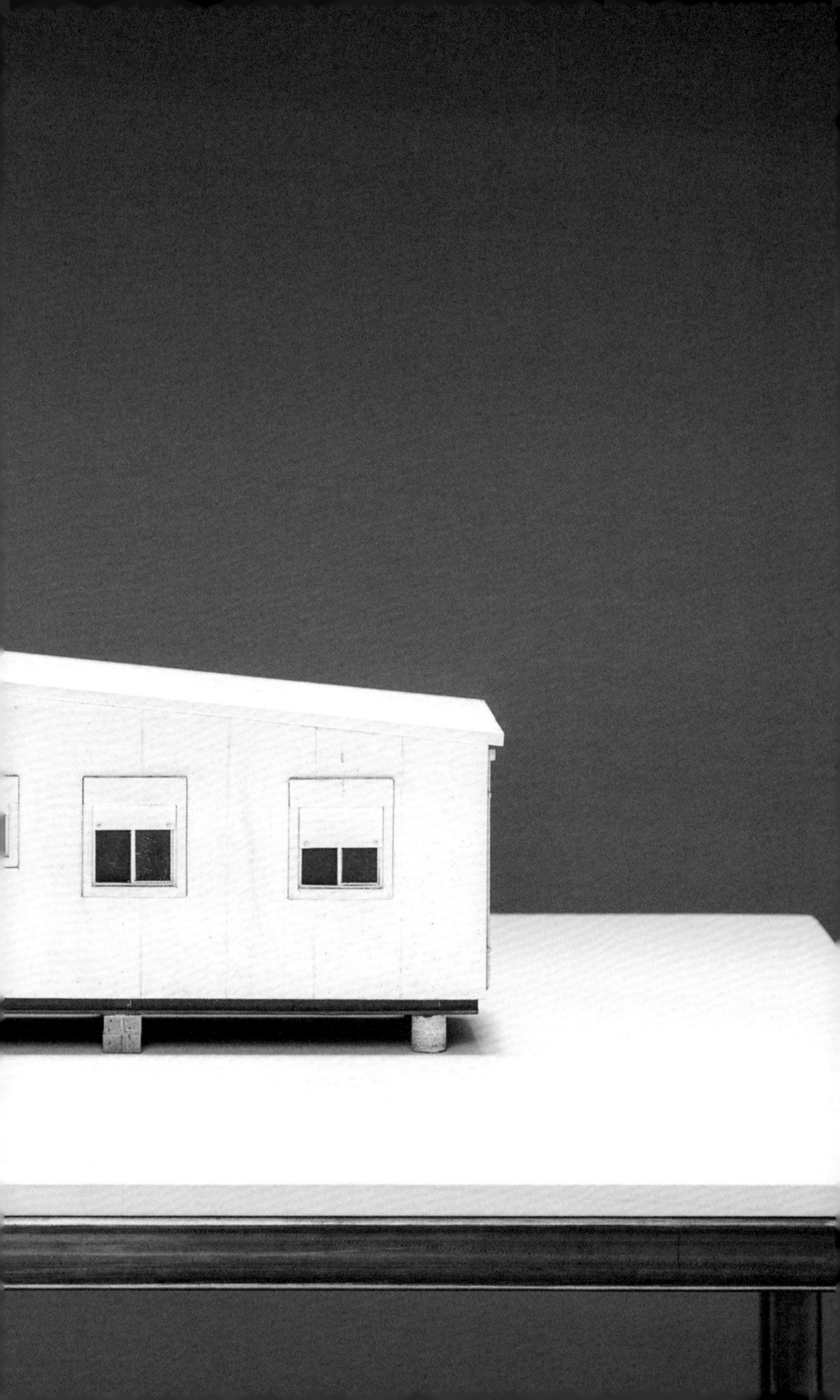

E47

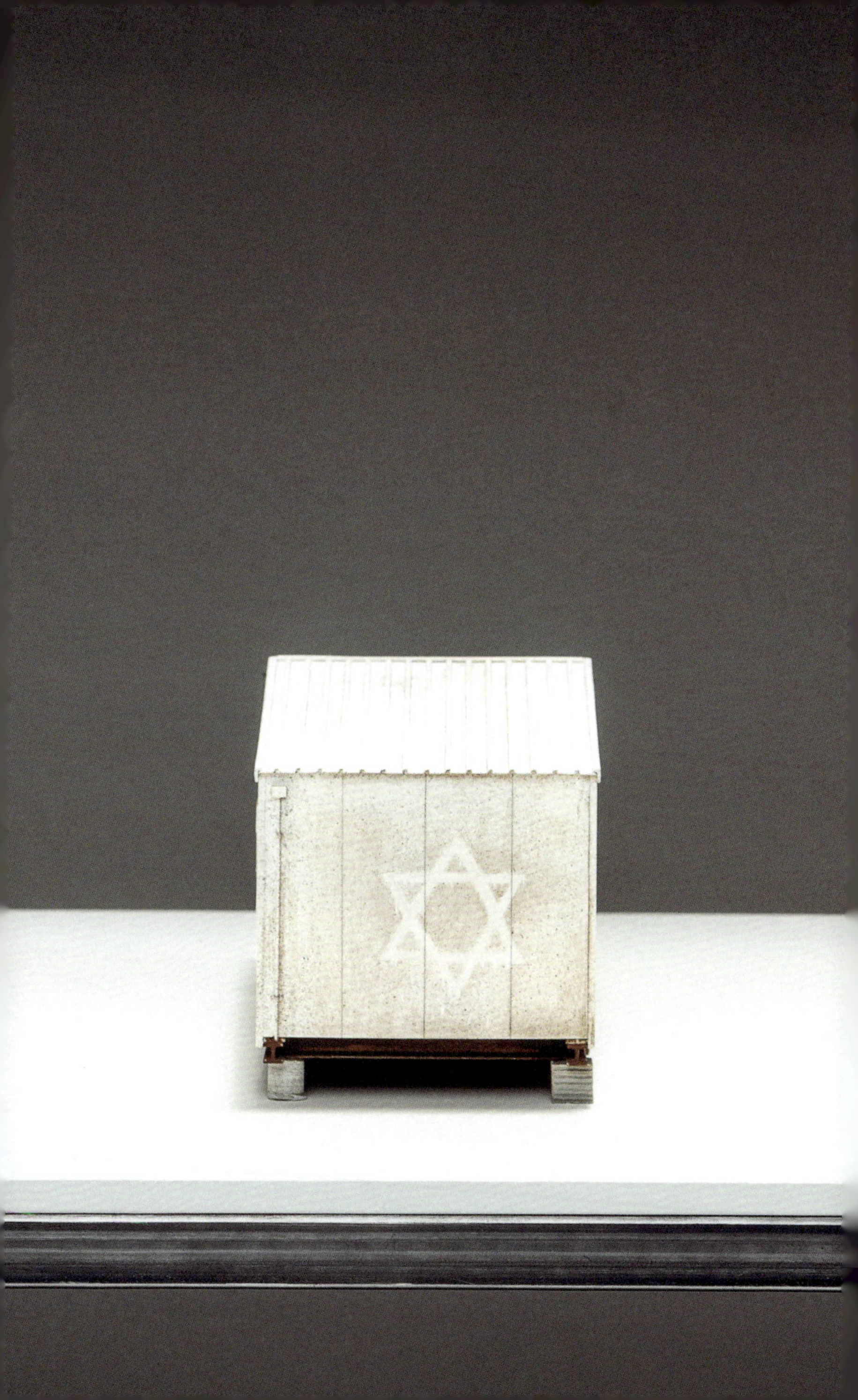

*Amona*, 2018–19

# This Land Is My Land, This Land Is My Land

## *Sabrina Orah Mark*

My son whose name is Land, and my other son whose name is Land leave on a bus the color of figs to fight in the Gentle War. I fill two small pouches with Land and Land's baby teeth and sew the pouches into the lining of their soft, pink uniforms. "For good luck," I say. I give them each a peanut butter and jelly sandwich wrapped in wax paper, a kiss on the forehead, and fresh, cold water in a blue canteen. Mothers are allowed to watch the Gentle War on television. It's the last television. The one in the Laundromat perched high in the corner like an old, stuffed dove. Some days I watch and some days I sleep, or get my nails done, or write letters to famous writers. Today I want to be a good mother so I go to "Nowhere Suds" to watch Land and Land arrive on the sunny battlefield arm in arm. The enemy skips by. "What a war," says a mother. I recognize her from the supermarket. Her kid, whose name is L.F. (short for "Lost and Found"), was born without eyes but now he has eyes. "It's so boring," says the mother. "Nothing happens." My Lands are gathering stones and placing one stone on top of the other, as one might carefully stack a pile of bodies. There are six other mothers. Two are knitting. I never learned how to knit, though I did have a dream last night I knit a scarf for Land and Land. Blue and brown and long like a river. I separate Land and Land's darks and whites. I wash everything on cold and delicate. I look up at the television. Land is napping under a tree. Land is drawing what looks like a heart from here.

"How," asks a mother, "can you tell Land and Land apart?" Her mouth is too small, but I answer her anyway:

> *Land is happier than Land. Land is a worrier. Land has a furrow in his brow so deep I could grow daffodils, lavender, ranunculus, heliotrope. Land is quiet and forgetful. When Land laughs Land laughs his head off. Land cries more easily than Land. Land is a better speller. Land likes salty, while Land likes sweet. Land is the part of Earth not covered by water. Land has a birthmark that floats over his lip, like the dot over an i. Land has a bruise from yesterday. Land sleeps in yellow pajamas covered in twinkling stars. Land lost two teeth. Land lost three. For his birthday, Land wants ninety-nine pennies. And Land wants a caramel cake with strawberries all over. And Land once chewed the whole erasure off his pencil while he should've been writing a sentence about the moon. And Land has trouble falling asleep.*

At the end of the day, Land and Land come home on the same fig colored bus. The children wave. Goodbye, Land. Goodbye, Land. Land and Land rush towards me with their arms wide, bury their small bodies in the folds of my skirt, and cry big mossy, ancient tears. What they have seen fighting the Gentle War no child should ever see.

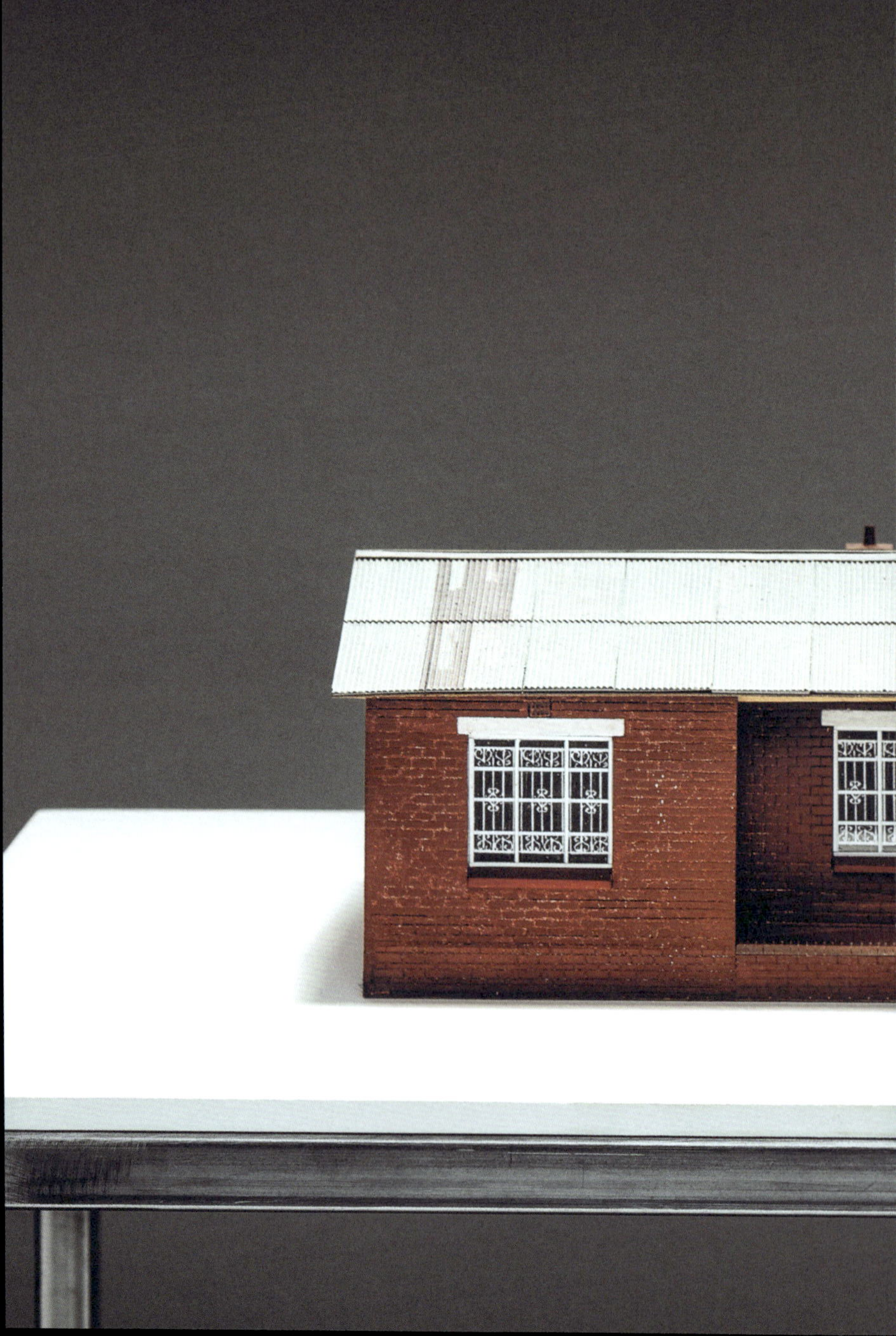

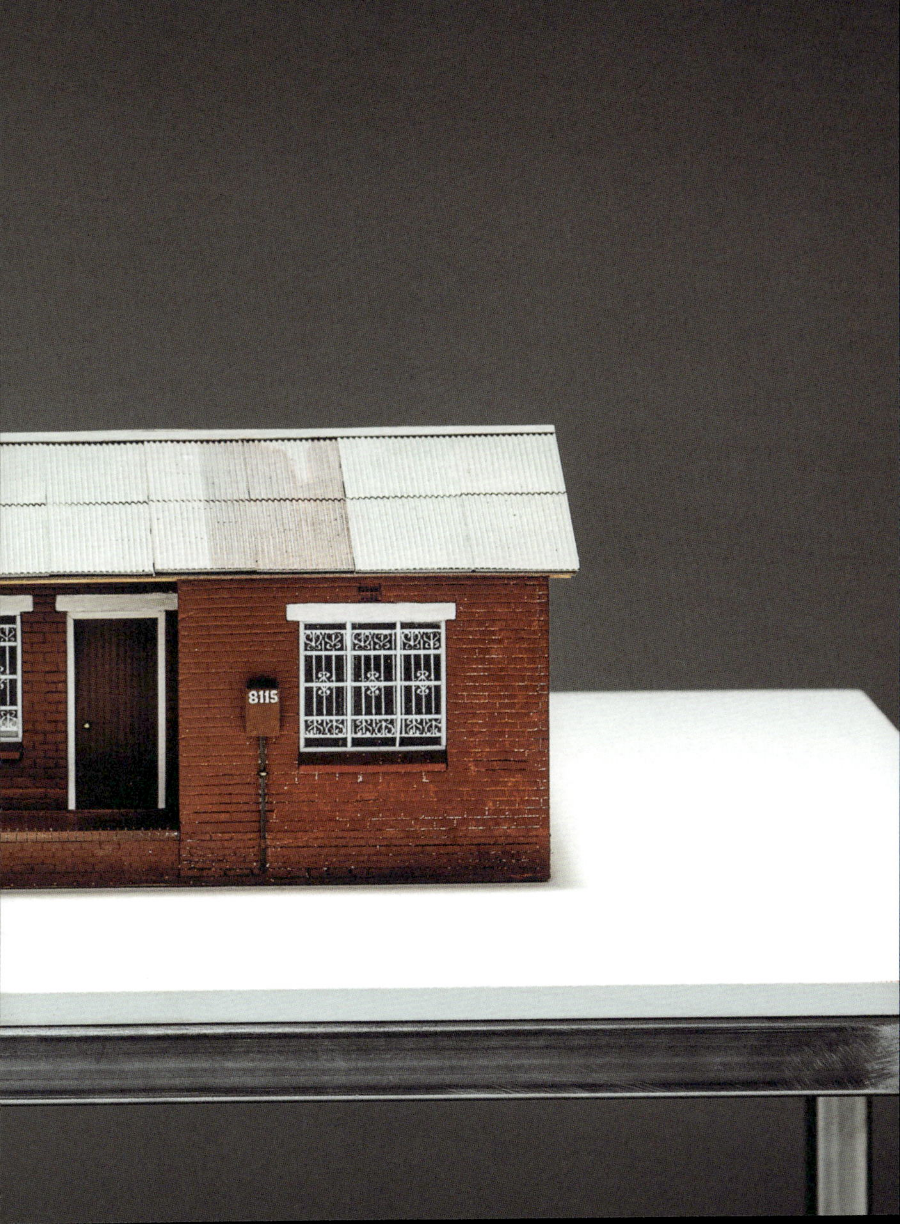
8115

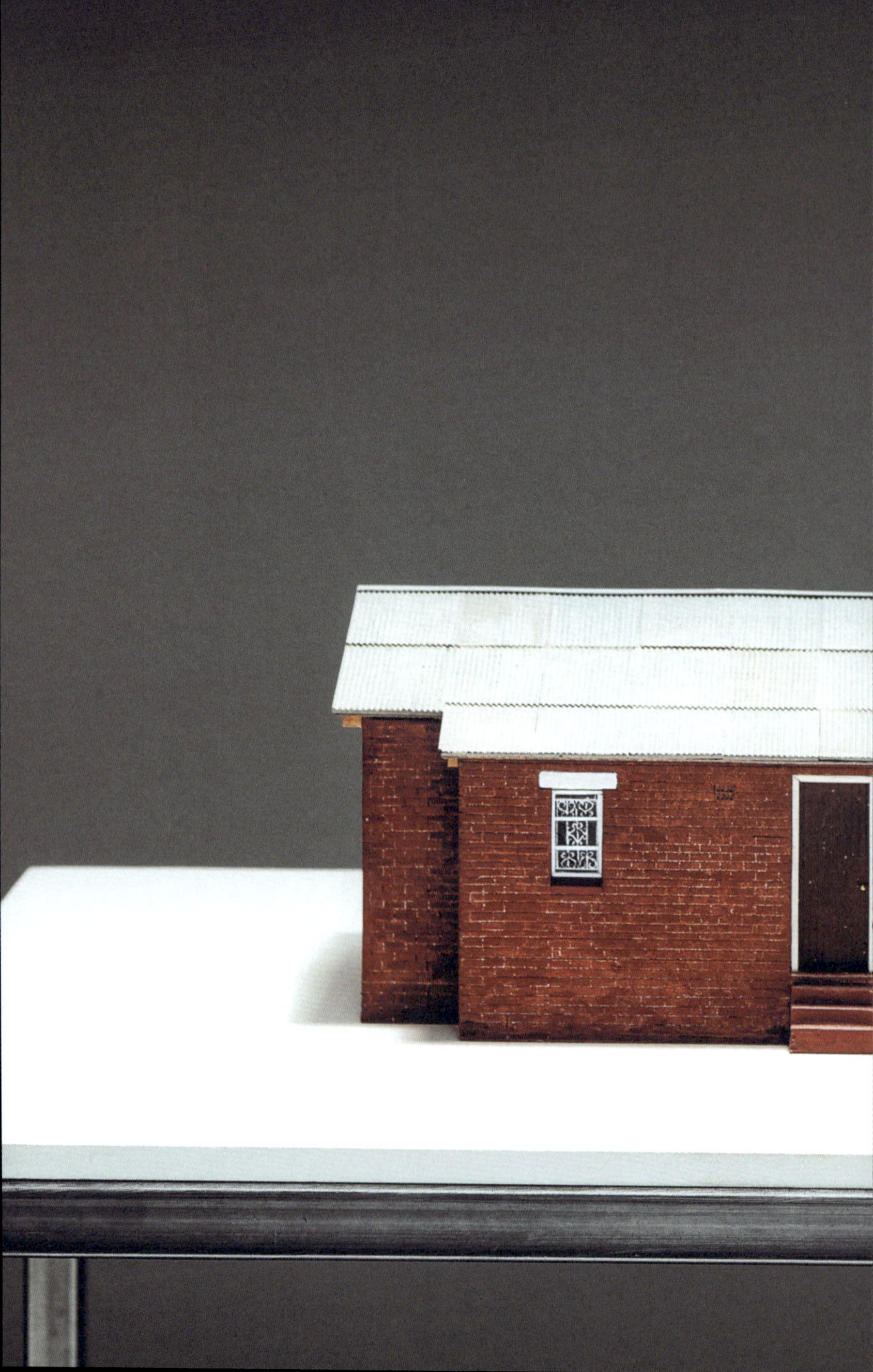

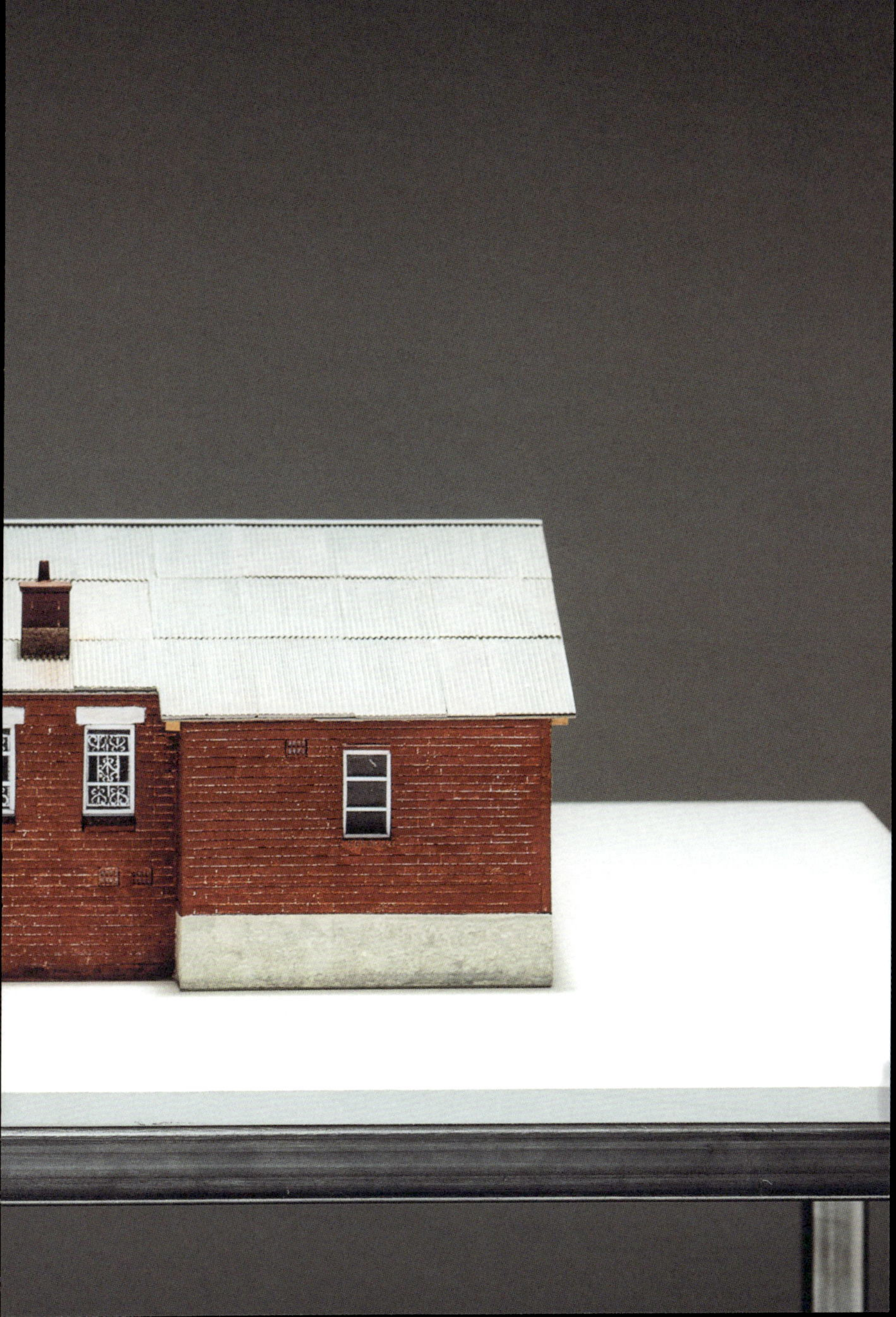

*8115 Vilakazi Street*, 2018–19

# Walking through History

## *Achmat Dangor*

The two young boys are in Mayfair, a white neighbourhood known for its hostility to blacks and Indians especially. Funny, Idris is often mistaken for a white child and would have had no trouble walking through these streets if he was on his own. Now, side by side with his darker brother, they look like just another couple of "Koelie" kids trespassing in a white area. They hurry on.

The sun is sinking very quickly and they still have another "Boere" area, Brixton, to pass through. It is "working class" and from the conversations they've overheard among the adults at home, this means that it is even rougher than Mayfair. At the top of Brixton Hill, they encounter a group of Afrikaner students on their way home from a rugby match. The two brothers walk along as if nothing is amiss, until one of the white kids shouts, "Koelies!"

The two boys start running, and don't stop until they reach Fuel Road, where the white area ends and "Western Native Township" begins. They slow down when they've crossed Fuel Road. They are within the psychologically "safe" borders of a black area, and stroll along, until Adam realises how late it is. He suggests they take a shortcut through Western.

– Are you mad? his brother Idris asks.

The place borders Sophiatown and is notorious for its gangs. Suddenly Adam starts acting the big brother and explains their options, as he sees them. They could walk through Coronationville, called Corrie in local slang, all the way to Westbury station. But that isn't any safer.

– Remember those kids near the Corrie Hospital?

He recounts the number of times they got chased when passing by the Coronation Hospital, and reminds Idris of the stories their friends have told them about being caught, and brutally attacked for no reason at all.

– Those Corrie "lighties" are mad!

Idris agrees, reluctantly, even though he knows that his brother is exaggerating. He is aware of how Adam loves exploring areas they rarely venture into, especially if it is a place their parents have warned them to avoid. They make their way through the smoke-filled dusk, two boys who obviously do not belong. Their clothes, well-cut serge trousers, expensive shoes, leftovers from a more opulent time, set them apart. So does the way they carry themselves. They have not yet learned to "bump," that self-protective local gait, shoulders hunched, one leg flung forward off the other's pinion, just like someone with an elaborate limp. Thank goodness, no one bothers them, and they cross over Steytler Street without incident, and then Hamilton, distant frontiers their parents have forbidden them from crossing.

Idris is becoming irritated; his elation has worn off and he feels that his brother is using the opportunity to satisfy his crazy need to see new things and new places all the time. He suggests that they walk up toward Wanderers Avenue, where the big houses are, and cross over at the Newclare Station bridge. But Adam ignores him and changes the subject.

– Hey, what are we going to tell Mummy and Daddy about why we walked home? Adam asks.

– I'll tell them the truth. Uncle Baboo was angry with us for some reason.

– You mean we really tell them that our Uncle Baboo dumped us because he was angry that I saw him with his "Aunty?"

– What Aunty? What are you talking about?

– What do you think he was doing in that flat? Screwing a woman!

Adam looks at his brother's astonished face, and realizes that his brother did not see what their Uncle Baboo was doing. Now he'll understand why the crazy Uncle got mad when Adam joked about the "naked Aunty," and threw them out of his car.

– Listen, don't say anything, we'll take our hiding if that's what we get, Idris says.

– What, I'm going to take a hiding because of Uncle Baboo? Nah!

– Hey, you know what he's like, he'll make us pay until the day we die.

They walk in silence towards the tunnel; it is dark now and the feeble streetlights make almost no difference. Braziers glow comfortingly in backyards, despite the heat. Most of homes here are too small to light fires indoors, so people cook their meals outside. The smell of roasting meat, of stiff porridge and boiled cabbage fills the air. Despite the unwelcome odour of this smelly vegetable, they both feel hungry and pick up their pace again. Their mother would be home from work by now, busy preparing supper, usually a stew, or meat and potatoes. Then the whole family has to sit around the table and "eat like decent human beings."

How boring it all becomes. Somehow the lives of the people they pass seem more adventurous, filled with noise and warmth; children laugh and play outside, while their parents sit back and watch.

Adam wonders what it would be like not to live in a proper house, with brick walls and slanting tin roofs, and in a "decent" area like their own?

# Missing Mandela

## *Mohale Mashigo*

Thandi lied to her mother about where she was going. It was easier to say she was visiting a friend. That was better than saying "I'm going to find Nelson Mandela, so I don't fail English." What was supposed to be a fairly simple essay was now getting in the way of an ambitious goal she had set for herself: Nothing lower than a B on her second term report. If anything, she felt like Ms Attwell was targeting her because she wasn't a happy-clappy frothing-at-the-mouth believer of the fabled rainbow nation. Why else would she be so offended by a silly essay?

"Thandi, this is a very confusing essay. I know you can do better than this." Her teacher was shuffling papers on her desk. She had asked Thandi to remain in class after the last school bell of the day had rung. "What's so confusing about it?" Thandi picked up her essay that was decorated with a bright D on the cover. The title 'Mandela: Missing Man or Mythical Man?' was bold and underlined. "You know why," still the teacher's eyes didn't move from her desk. "I'm giving you a chance to rewrite it this weekend. I want it first thing on Monday morning."

The small red brick house reminded Thandi of her own grandmother's house in the township of Mofulo. No matter, where you were in Soweto, you would find tiny houses like the one she was standing in front of. The three big windows in the front of the house made it look smaller. Thandi's grandmother would have yelled at the people who were standing in the doorway. "Nobody enters through that door! Go around and knock on the kitchen door like you have manners."

There were two buses parked outside the small red-bricked house. One of them was so obviously a tourist bus. The passengers were all standing outside the house taking or posing for photos. "Crass," Thandi muttered under her breath. The other bus was old with strange decorations around the windows. "Who knows what tourism gimmick they've come up with now?" was what Thandi thought when she walked towards the backdoor of the house. Saturdays were always busy, no matter what the season, many people had 'visit 8115 Vilakazi Street' on their bucket list.

The bride was smiling as the tourist's cameras took in all her beauty. Although Thandi didn't understand a word of what was being spoken, she knew that the observers were praising her beauty. A crowd had gathered around the four steps leading to the back door of the red brick house. The bride and her bridesmaids must have been passengers of the old PUTCO bus with decorations around the window. Instead of focusing on the bullet holes on the walls or memorabilia inside, people wanted a closer look at the young bride and her three bridesmaids.

The tiara is what amazed Thandi, it looked like an exact replica with a veil cascading down the brides back. Not even the guide understood the significance of the four women. "Please tell us ... are you getting married?" The accent sounded German. "Is this performance art?" It was a hurried American voice that asked the second question. Many others shouted requests and inquiries as the bride smiled at them. One of the bridesmaids finally said something. She brushed the short lace sleeve of the dress that matched her two friends next to her. Her white gloves were ill-fitting so she kept pulling them up to the elbow. "My sister is getting married today. Before we go to church, she wanted to see Mandela House." There was applause from three Chinese tourists.

Thandi couldn't take her eyes off the bride who was nonchalantly sitting on the red steps with her wedding gown just barely touching the red paving. She was giddy. "How could I not come to the house of my hero? I live two streets away. We start here and then off to church." She giggled and smiled once more for her newly found fans. "Welcome to Soweto. You're very lucky to see where a hero lived." The bridesmaids hurried behind her to pick up the train of her dress as she walked into the house to take selfies. Long after the bride had left in her old decorated bus, Thandi walked away from 8115 Vilakazi Street.

On the taxi ride back home, she searched for the wedding photo. "I knew it," she whispered. A young Nelson Mandela was smiling broadly holding the hands of his bride who wore a veil attached to a tiara. There were two adults named Mandela who lived in that house. The Bus Bride had Winnie Mandela's wedding gown and bridesmaid's dresses recreated for her special day. Thandi looked outside and hoped Miss Attwell would like her new essay about a Missing Mandela; worthy of paeans penned by proud brides in old PUTCO buses.

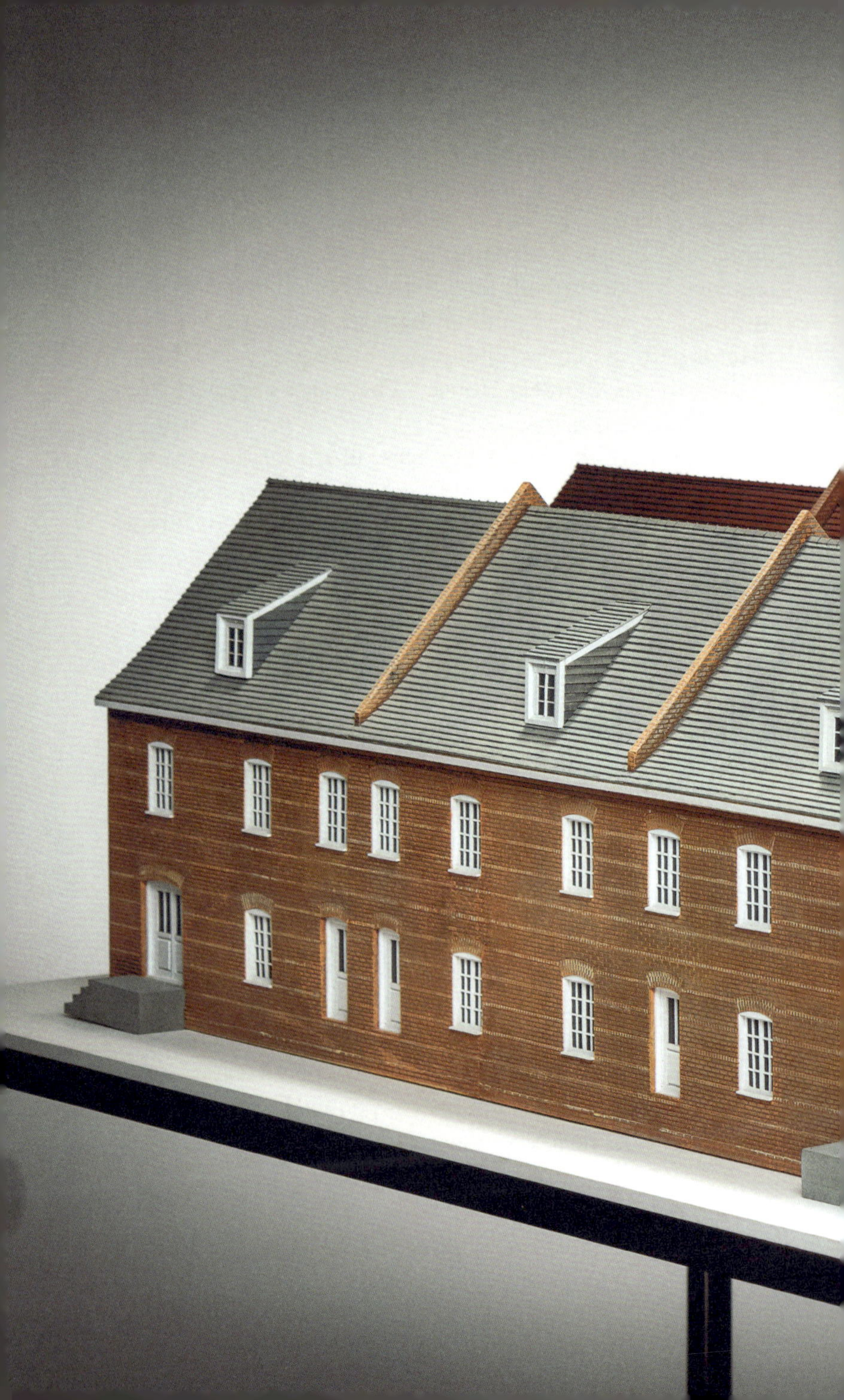

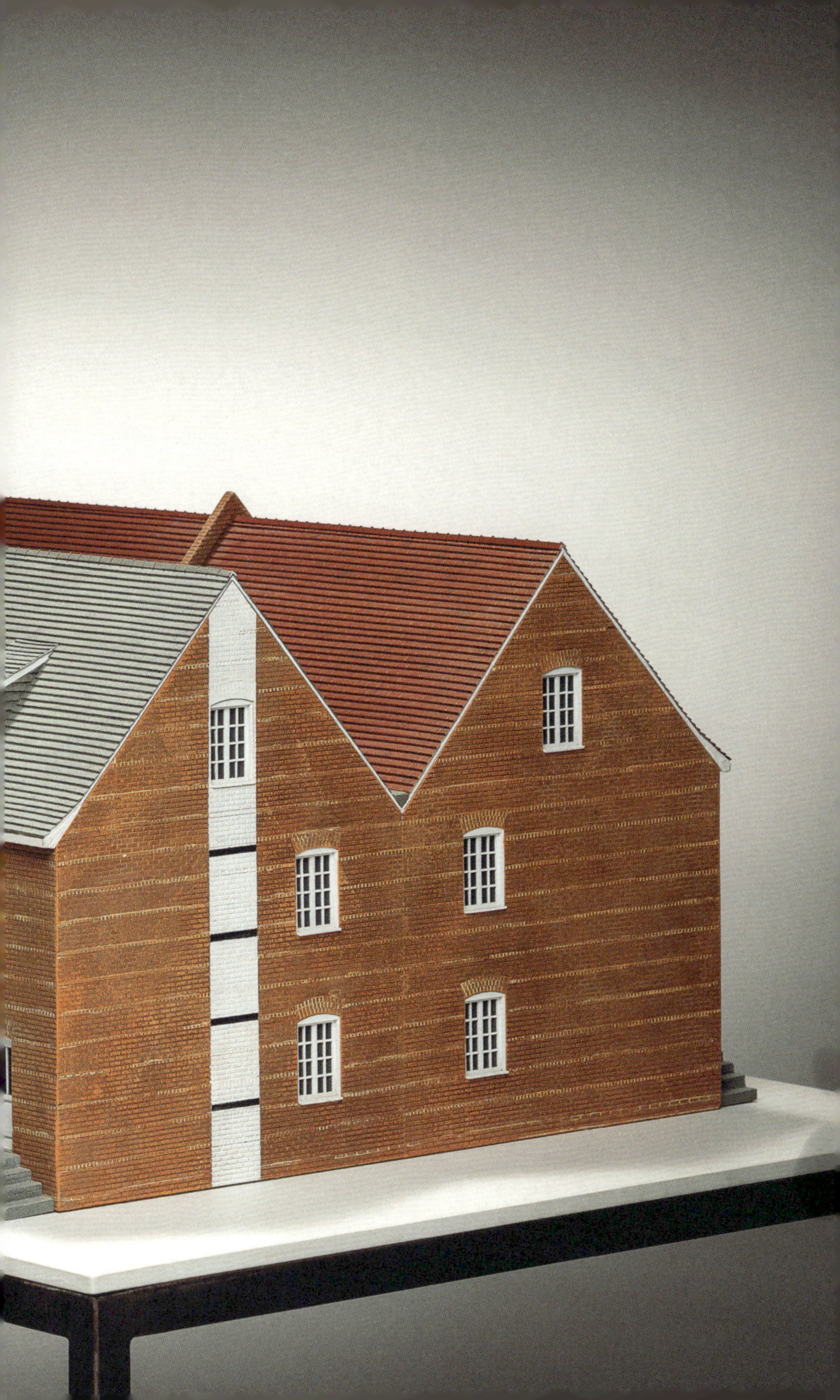

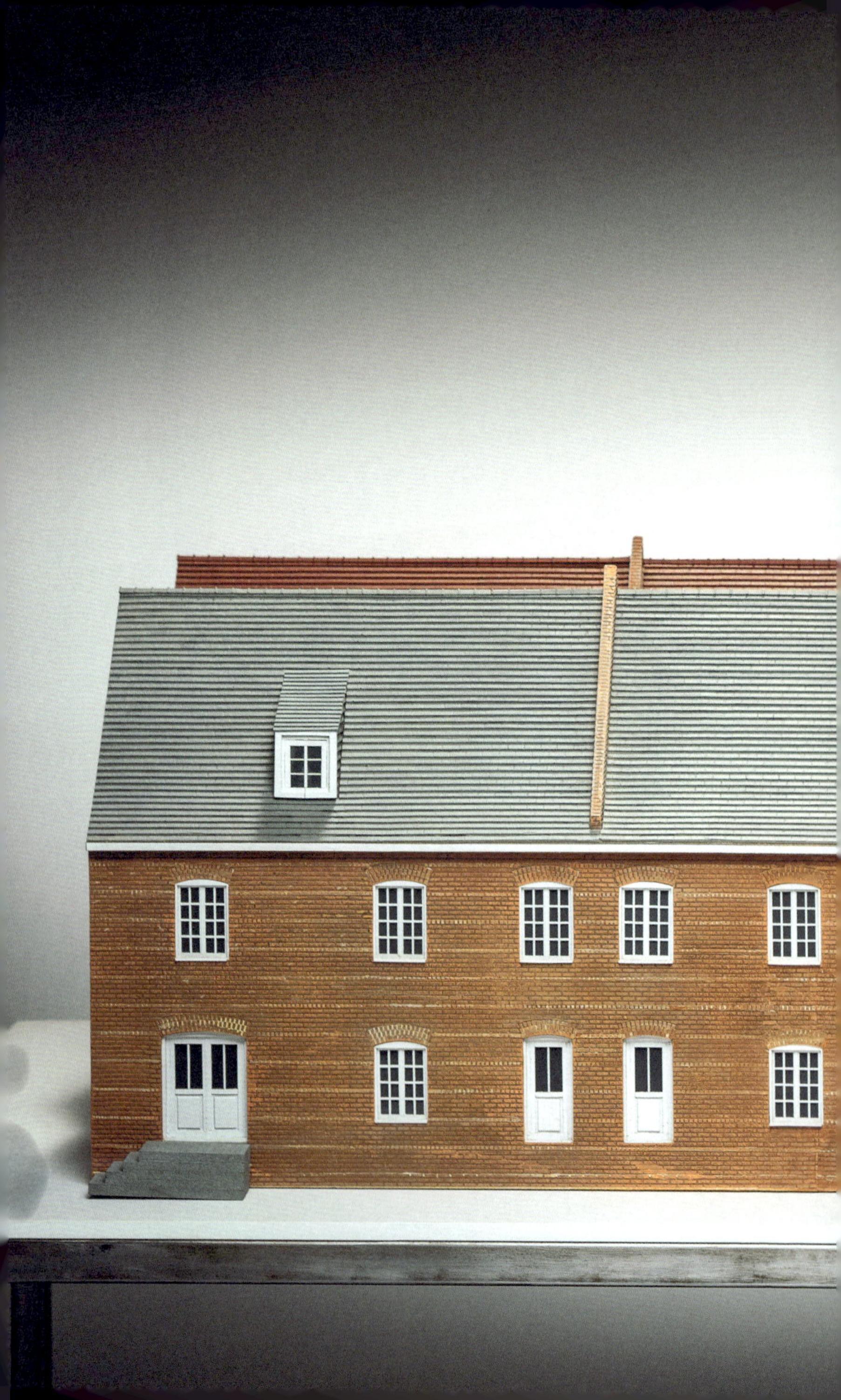

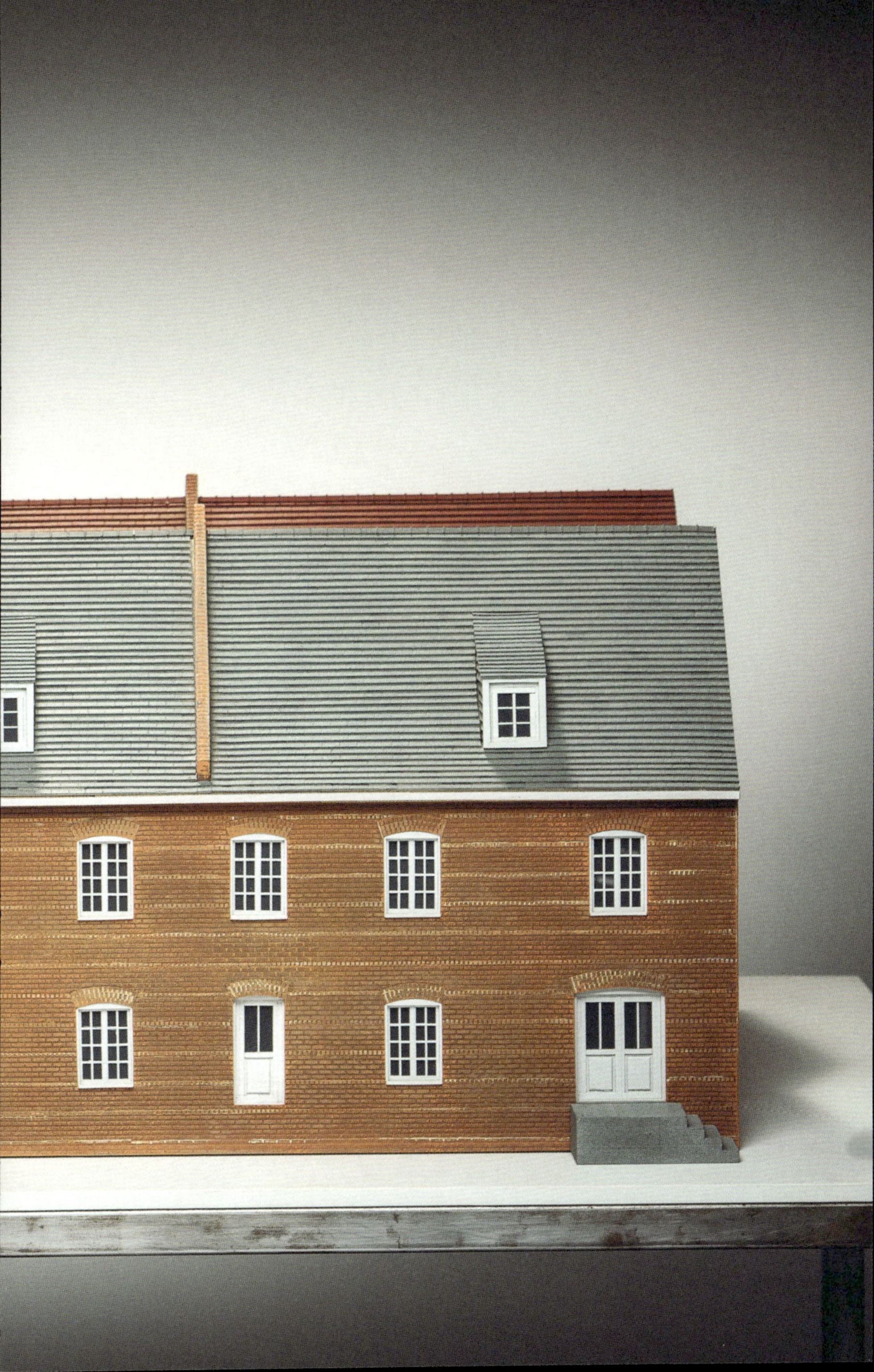

*German Village*, 2014–15

# German Village

## *Amina Cain*

The desert is quiet and something gets carried out. There I am in my alabaster dress out on the rocks. I've gone to the rocks, even though I was told to stay in German Village. I am half Mormon, and look remotely like I live in Berlin, the envy of everyone here. No one else has had the desert, and German Village, imprinted on them quite as I have. The Utah desert and German Village—they have gotten carried out—on me.

Look at this heavy bed with its heavy pillows. I don't like a heavy blanket. I feel good out in the rocks; there is salt in the air and the salt is healthy. My skin absorbs it. Even when I'm inside, I sit next to an open window so I can breathe it in. I do my thinking there. I do my language lessons. When I'm cleaning, I clean those areas of the apartment the most. I feel strongly next to the windows. And if someone could see me from a long way off, filling the window in that way? When I try to talk about this to the others, no one cares.

* * *

Away from German Village, I see a strange weed in the sand and I bend over it. And then we both become humps of life, a good shape for living. The stalk bends over into the shape of a rainbow, which is a shape I hardly see. I bend over while holding onto the chair that is next to the window. I run in the sand. No one else runs here; they think I am trying to escape. I am.

My life deepened when someone brought me herbs, someone who pitied me, and it deepened more when I began to grow them in a little patch next to our building. Now I have salt, and I have fresh herbs all the time. I am trying to fully cultivate my home life next to the open window; I want to see if it is possible. I lay marjoram, tarragon, and parsley out on the windowsill to dry. Their stalks are slim; they have fine green leaves. It changes the apartment. Now even when I lie down on the heavy bed with the heavy blanket on top of me, I have the sense of the salt and the herbs, and the window and the desert. In this way I am rejecting German Village, pushing its imprint off. My soul wants to see the salt lake. I light my candle at night and meditate on the inland sea.

All night when I sleep, my face is next to the herbs, even if only spiritually. They overlap, my face and the herbs, beating like two hearts, then one heart, and become what they were meant to be. I can wake up and look at the herbs. I can meditate on them with my eyes closed. They appear, right where my third eye should be.

But this can't go on forever. I know I'm not long for this world, and neither is my hated German Village. All of us die, but I'll die sooner. Sometimes it grieves me, but there's nothing I can do. Sometimes I feel so afraid, I fear I will die of that.

Regardless, I wake up fresh and very much alive. The herbs and the salt do this to me. I am able to go through my days with a pleasurable feeling as though I were living somewhere else, somewhere Mediterranean. This goes on for several weeks. Still, it nags at me.

* * *

Back on the rocks, at night this time, so I brought my candle. I went almost without thinking. How nice the rocks are with candlelight on them, how particularly sharp and pointed with weeds growing among them here and there. I push my shirtsleeves up to my elbows. My long skirt brushes against the strange weeds. Here is an insect with a very hard body and antennas that twitch constantly around, touching the rocks. Here is a spider, much smaller than the other, but entirely furred and waiting behind one of the rocks, ready to pounce. I know I shouldn't interfere, but I don't want the spider to kill the hard-shelled insect. Kill me instead. Maybe this is a good way to die.

I won't bend over them and I won't run; I'll turn away and let them move toward their destinies. I will try to turn toward mine, burning brightly like my candle. I'll lie down on the rocks and let them make their choices. And if they don't choose to kill me, if they kill each other instead, at least the rocks are sharp. I will let my third eye touch one the way the hard-shelled insect touches them with its antenna, but harder.

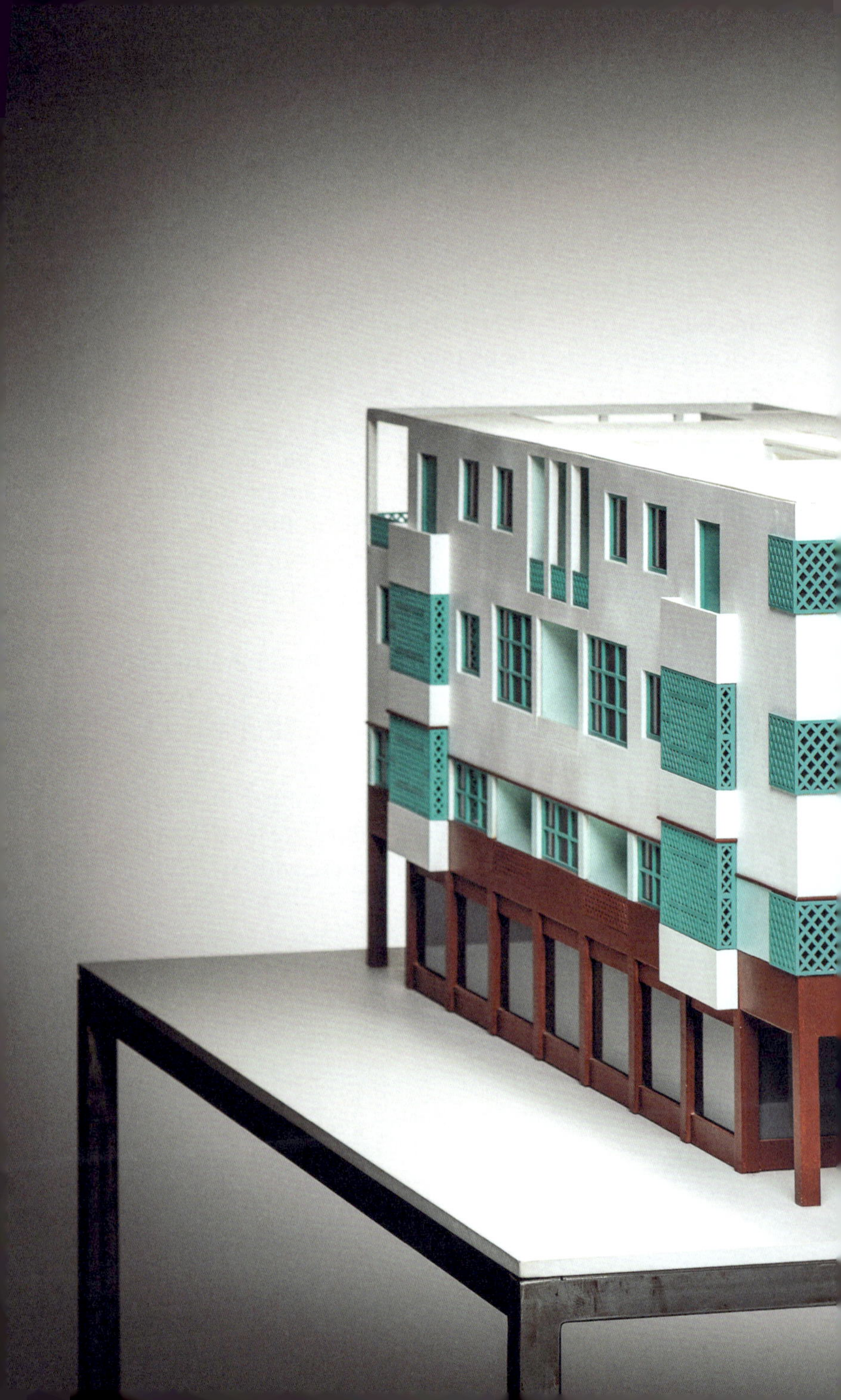

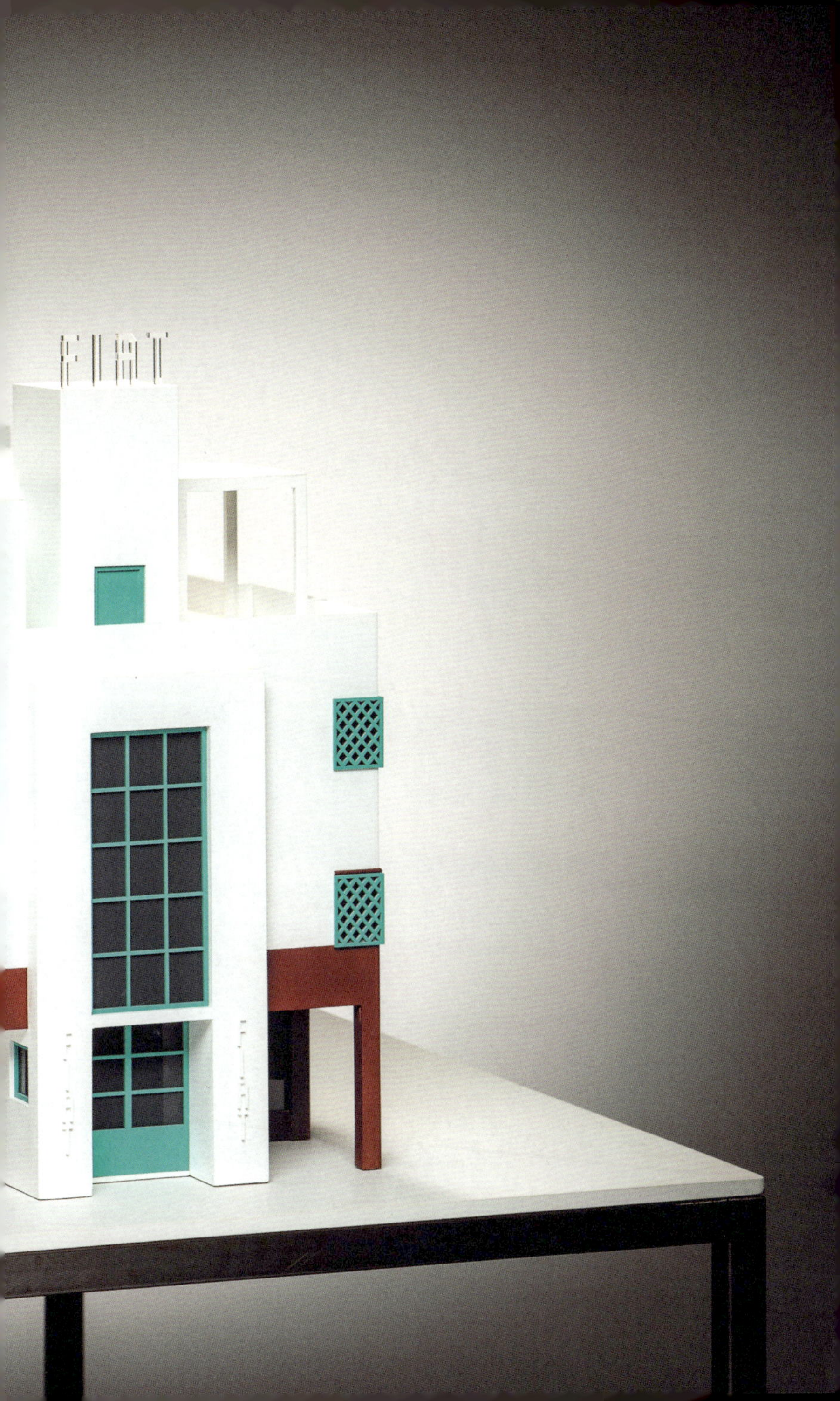
FIAT

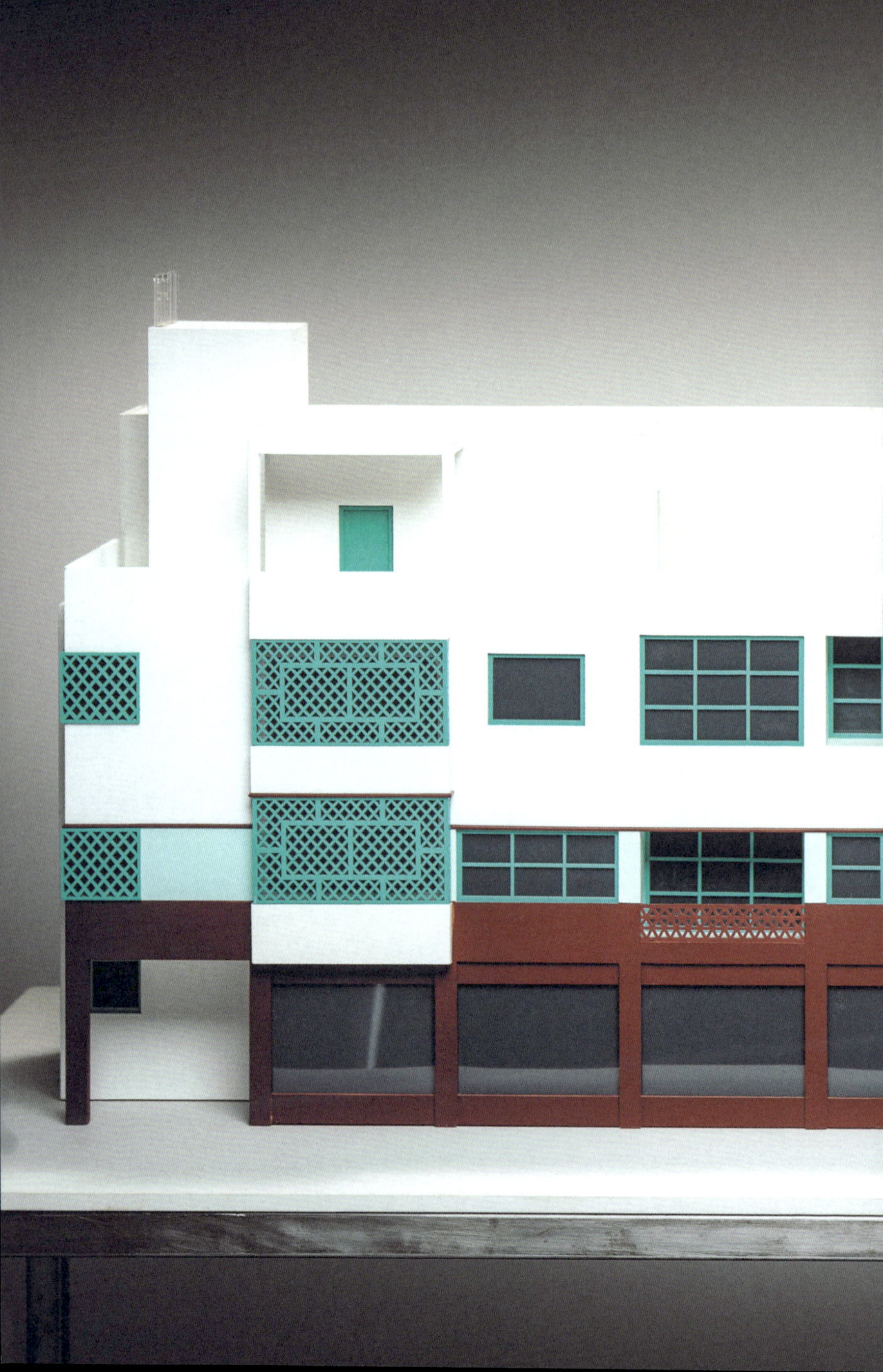

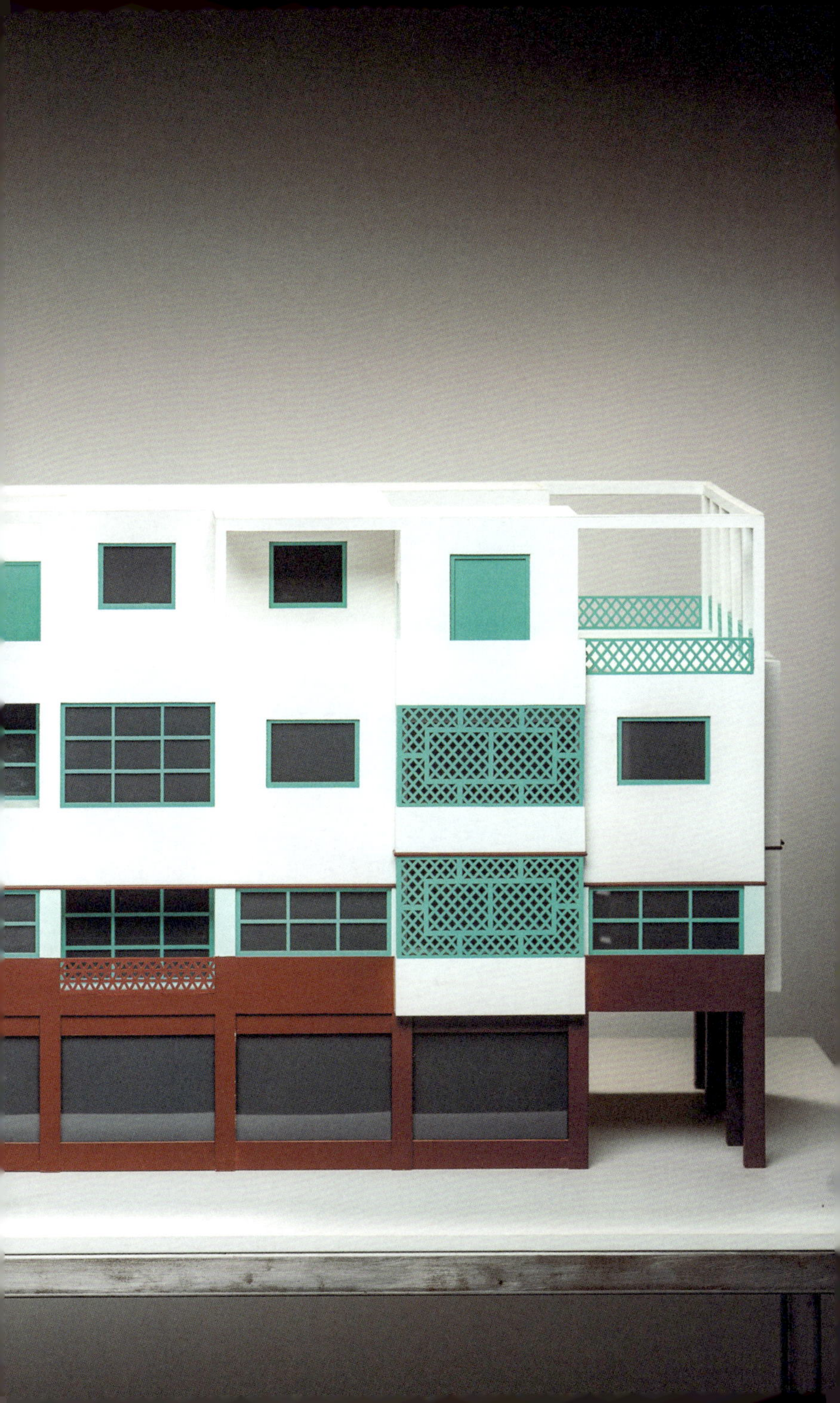

*Tripoli,* 2015

# In a Space We Inhabit, in a Time that Inhabits Us

## *Ibrahim al-Koni*

*The Qaramanli Dynasty ruled Tripolitania 1711–1833 CE.*

### 1

"The treasure I inherited from my father isn't the throne—as the masses believe—but his testaments."

The Pasha's companion smiled and replied, "We say in France that a man won't outstrip his ancestors unless he cherishes their testaments."

The Pasha ignored M. Jardin's comment and completed his own thought: "I won't be exaggerating if I say that one of his most important testaments was respect for the treaty with France."

As if to himself, M. Jardin murmured, "Did I hear the Pasha use the word 'treaty,' or was that just my imagination?"

"Yes indeed; Ahmad the Great considered our relationship with your country to be a treaty and not a transaction—unlike our relationships with other countries."

"I'm happy that the Pasha has inherited from his father a treasure greater than sovereignty and of greater importance even than testaments; it is wisdom!"

"To demonstrate my intention to act on my father's

admonition, I plan to send an emissary to His Excellency the King of France."

"I will be happy to convey to His Excellency, Your Honor's intention to dispatch an envoy to him!"

"I wouldn't think heeding a testament is a feat were it not so difficult to restrain a people's appetite for raids on the high seas."

"This is because seafaring is the only trade they know, Your Honor the Pasha."

"You may grasp what it means to suppress a people's deeply ingrained appetite."

The diplomat commented with a grimace: "Anyone who suppresses a person's work suppresses his message, and someone who suppresses a man's message suppresses his happiness. Therefore, a person who restrains a man's happiness exposes his own life to danger!"

The Pasha rose and gazed at the awesome sea, which stretched from the foot of the fortress for an apparently infinite distance. He remarked, "You don't know how much these wretches love this monster!"

"I can imagine, Your Honor the Pasha!"

"They don't just yearn for a tryst with this beloved to search for treasures, as imbeciles assume. The treasures found on the open sea are merely a pretext. Believe me!"

"I do, Your Honor the Pasha."

"The sea isn't merely a body of water; it is life itself!"

The diplomat prepared to leave, and the Pasha saw him off with a wan smile. Then he objected before the French representative reached the door: "But you haven't asked the name of my emissary to His Excellency."

M. Jardin paused, and the Pasha added, "It is Mr. Ahmad Hasan Kahiya!"

## 2

On the evening news spread that Ahmad Hasan Kahiya had been chosen as the Pasha's emissary to His Excellency the King of France, a certain father told his son: "If Ahmad Kahiya succeeds in reaching the court of the King of the Christians, all our dreams will evaporate!"

They sat facing each other on wooden chairs in the family's orchard in al-Manshiya, enjoying the stillness of the fields during the brief winter twilight.

The father looked at his son and then cast his gaze over the clusters of olive trees lined up in columns, which were interrupted first by orange, pomegranate, and fig trees, and then by date palms. He said: "A man is nothing but a dream and ceases to be a man if the dream dies in his heart!"

* * *

"Does the offspring of Hasan Kahiya have hair like Samson's, an Achilles' heel?"

The son reflected. He rose and took a few paces in the orchard. Then he retraced his steps. He stopped abruptly and shouted: "Mahmud Bey!"

The father stared at him apprehensively. The son added, "Ahmad Hasan Kahiya is Mahmud Bey's close friend!"

The father reflected. He too rose and paced through the orchard. Then he stopped and exclaimed, "We've found the key!"

The father smiled, gazed into his son's eyes, and took a deep breath as the plot's elements fell into place in his mind. He said, "Mahmud Bey is truly a dervish, but legally he has a stronger claim to the throne, because he is a son of the Great Pasha. He has never attached any importance to the throne because he's a dervish! People, though, aren't dervishes and have been whispering in Mahmud Bey's ear that he is entitled to the throne, and his dear friend Ahmad Kahiya is among them. No, he first among them."

The two men exchanged a long look. All at once they burst into laughter. This was a restrained, terrifying chortle that echoed through the gloom that crept through the neighboring fields to embrace the fruit trees.

3

While Muhammad Pasha al-Qaramanli gazed at the sea from a balcony of the palace and wondered why Adam's spawn were keen to embark on rash adventures, the Bambara sprite was entering the city's walls through Bab al-Bahr, the Sea Gate, prodding a gray jenny laden with two barrels of water.

The sun had just dispelled dawn's gloom, and watchmen were on the scene, opening the awe-inspiring gates that protected the city on four sides like legendary amulets the Unknown had erected at unknown times—not to defend the city against invaders' guile nor to protect it against the machinations of the jinn, who preferred to wreak havoc on earth at dusk.

The watchmen were accustomed to welcome at their gates, at dawn every day, the water-seller. This ill-tempered fellow had always seemed one of the storied ghosts that prowled the city throughout the night. To ward off their evils, ancient peoples had erected fortresses.

The water sprite had draped a gray cloak, which was woven from camel hair, around him as if to announce winter's premature onslaught, but this cloth covered only his chest and haunches, leaving his knees and shanks bare. He reached Sahat al-Rukham with his grey donkey and stopped opposite the Arch of Marcus Aurelius to murmur an incomprehensible curse that may have been a gibberish phrase inherited from distant ancestors in the forestlands beyond the Sahara or perhaps an ancient pagan charm transmitted from his original homelands. Then he turned his beast of burden to the left to follow the street that led to the square where the French Consulate stood. There he roared with a voice that shook nearby walls: "Give me one *mahbub,* and I'll give you the secret of worldly life! A barrel for only one gold coin! Who but the water dervish would sell you a barrel of life for a metal coin?"

A passerby suppressed a laugh. A little girl looked down from a high window. A woman scoffed through a crack in a door. The guards at the door of the Consulate scolded him rudely and gestured for him to cross to the other side of the street. Pulling his wrap around his head, he forced the jenny to the far side of the street. But once they were a few steps beyond the watchmen, he drove her back to the side they had been on before. There he banged on a window, and a servant looked out. The fellow closed the window and came to open a panel of the door while the water-seller took down two barrels of water. The elderly African came outside. He was small in stature, and the hair on his temples was turning white. He approached and whispered into the sprite's ear words no one else would have understood. The water-seller responded with an ambiguous smile.

## 4

The calm inside this elegant residence, which adjoined the French Consulate, was eerie. A tall palm tree grew in the house's courtyard. The water sprite walked down the corridor leading to the bedrooms with the assurance of a man who knew what he wanted and how to get there. The elderly servant stayed behind, struggling with a water barrel, which bumped against the ceiling. Outside the wind howled with surprising agony, and rain pounded on the room's windows that overlooked the harbor to the north. Once inside this room, where silence, darkness, and opulence reigned, the sprite listened intently. At the end of an alcove on the north wall, he heard gentle snoring. He stared into the darkness and detected the wide, luxurious sleeping area, which was delimited by a diaphanous curtain. This love nest resembled the boudoir of a princess in *The Thousand and One Nights* or some other ancient legend. Holding his breath, he took a step and then a second toward this splendid alcove. Then he paused to examine the body that lay on the bed that imagination's nightgown draped. He discovered that two bodies were locked in such intimate embrace that they formed a single person.

He smiled, swallowed lasciviously, and approached the love nest. He gazed at the couple with eyeballs so lustful they almost leapt from their sockets.

His fearsome hands hovered over their bodies but remained suspended over their heads as if paralyzed. The appearance of the beautiful woman the man embraced stunned the sprite.

He told himself that the master of this house had every right to meet his Lord both satisfied and satisfying after embracing such a beautiful courtesan.

Why shouldn't he extend his hand to pluck this fruit of paradise, since the fates had placed it within his reach? Didn't people say destiny only grants us one opportunity to fulfill our wishes?

When his hands descended on the man's neck, he found it as brittle as straw. They sank into this flaccid neck, which resembled a cylinder of cheese. The man released a brief death rattle. His body quivered twice, a third time, and was lifeless.

Having finished off the male, he turned his attention to the beauty, who still lay beside her lover. She was hugging his left arm and had no idea she was embracing a corpse.

Gazing at her marble neck, he admired her golden complexion despite the darkness. Her body was half-naked and covered only by a sheet even more diaphanous than the gauzy curtain.

She seemed an immortal dream the fates were offering him then but certainly wouldn't again. He preferred to embrace of this dream instead of receiving the payment he had been promised for his deed. He would seize this dream now, even if that meant they offered his neck to the executioner on the morrow.

He didn't know how much time was consumed by his insane coupling with the beauty. What roused him from this delirium was a fierce pounding on the door.

The woman was screaming. She was screaming because she was bleeding. He stretched out his hand to silence her forever, just as he had silenced her lover, Mr. Ahmad, not long before.

## 7

In al-Manshiya, in the Pasha's summer orchard, the Pasha asked the aged gardener, "Tell me, Uncle Sulayman, if you were fated to sit in my place, which of my counselors would you believe?"

The old man replied, as if reading an answer inscribed on parchment, "May God protect me from being destined to sit in my master's place!"

The Pasha smiled as though he had expected this response. He looked up at the crests of the palm trees and said, "As the saying goes: the fates that dictate sovereignty are blind."

The old man was scanning the area around him for weeds and bent from time to time and stood back up as agilely as a much younger man. He said, "If the fates made this colossal blunder, I wouldn't believe any of those people my Master refers to as 'counselors.'"

"Why not?"

"Because counselors are incapable of speaking truth to power."

"Really?"

"Counselors are predisposed, Master, to embellish lies for the Sultan, not to tell the truth!"

A south wind belched summer's desert wind and set the tops of the trees humming with a mysterious melody. The Pasha sat up straighter in the chair, which had been crafted from unidentified types of wood imported from overseas, and asked, "If I won't hear the truth from my counselors, to whom should I listen?"

"My Master may listen to them but shouldn't believe what he hears."

The Pasha was silent for a time and gazed again at the crests of the palms. Then he said, "I inherited from my father one man who spoke the truth to me, but they have killed him without me knowing why."

"I was sure they would, Master."

"Why did they kill him?"

"Because they couldn't rule unless they eliminated him."

"I thought I'm the ruler, not them."

The old man smiled for the first time, disclosing toothless gums, and bent over to extirpate a weed.

The gardener's bold talk reminded the Pasha that people reported he belonged to a Sufi order and had been seen Friday evenings on the lanes of al-Manshiya with dervishes of the 'Aisawiya or Qadiriya orders, participating in what these Sufis refer to as a "Hadra." Was the spirit of a Sufi order speaking through him when he said such hurtful things? Don't people say that only dervishes speak the truth?

The Pasha asked, "If things are as you say, what should I do to succeed?"

Without missing a beat, the gardener replied, "Don't do anything!"

"What?"

"Why should my Master search far and wide for the truth when he carries it in his heart?"

"What are you saying?"

"I mean that my Master should consult his own heart, not those of others!"

"How can I turn my heart into a counselor?"

"Not one counselor—many counselors!"

The Pasha looked curious, and the old man added: "In seclusion!"

Then, as he bent over a plant, he added, "Had he not resorted to *khalwa*, to spiritual seclusion, your ancestor, al-Qaramanli, would not have become the Commander of the Believers and Ahmad the Great!"

## List of Illustrations
## *Rehousing*, 2012–19

*Gründbergstraße 22*, 2012
Medium-density fiberboard, wood, brass, plexiglass, polyurethane resin, PVC, acrylic paint
23.7 × 36.5 × 21.5 cm
Collection Marco Rossi, Turin
pp. 16–19

*Uncle Ho*, 2012
Wood, polyurethane resin, PVC, acrylic paint
20.4 × 32 × 24.5 cm
Collection Marco Rossi, Turin
pp. 32–35

*Villa tropicale*, 2012–13
Medium-density fiberboard, brass, plexiglass, PVC, acrylic paint
14 × 26.7 × 21.4 cm
Collection Marco Rossi, Turin
pp. 44–47

*Evergreen*, 2013
Wood, polyurethane resin, acrylic paint
23.2 × 30.5 × 23.2 cm
Collection Marco Rossi, Turin
pp. 52–55

*Heidegger*, 2014
Medium-density fiberboard, wood, brass, PVC, polyurethane resin, acrylic paint
22.5 × 26 × 36 cm
Collection Marco Rossi, Turin
pp. 66–69

*Oranienplatz*, 2014
Medium-density fiberboard, wood, polypropylene, PVC, acrylic paint
19 × 22 × 30 cm
Collection Marco Rossi, Turin
pp. 74–79

*101*, 2016
ABS, wood, polyurethane resin, PVC, steel, acrylic paint
21 × 30 × 24 cm
Courtesy of the artist
pp. 86–89

*Azraq*, 2016
Medium-density fiberboard, wood, plexiglass, polystyrene, polyurethane resin, PVC, acrylic paint
16 × 31 × 22 cm
Courtesy of the artist
pp. 106–09

*Dome*, 2016
Medium-density fiberboard, wood, plexiglass, polyurethane resin, PVC, acrylic paint
18 × 45.5 × 45.5 cm
Courtesy of the artist
pp. 116–19

*Holdout*, 2016
Medium-density fiberboard, plexiglass, polystyrene, polyurethane resin, PVC, acrylic paint, watercolour
27.5 × 13 × 30 cm
Courtesy of the artist
pp. 130–35

*Amona*, 2018–19
Medium-density fiberboard, plexiglass, polystyrene, polyurethane resin, PVC, steel, acrylic paint
11.3 × 33.3 × 10.5 cm
Courtesy of the artist
pp. 144–49

*8115 Vilakazi Street,* 2018–19
Formica, medium-density fiberboard, wood, brass, plexiglass, polyurethane resin, PVC, acrylic paint
11.5 × 34.4 × 26 cm
Courtesy of the artist
pp. 154–57

Tables:
steel, plywood, acrylic paint
100 × 60 × 60 cm

*German Village,* 2014–15
Medium-density fiberboard, plexiglass, PVC, polyurethane resin, wood, acrylic paint
34.5 × 90.5 × 57.5 cm
Courtesy of the artist and Guido Costa Projects, Turin
pp. 166–69

*Tripoli,* 2015
Medium-density fiberboard, plexiglass, PVC, wood, acrylic paint
48 × 104 × 32.2 cm
Courtesy of the artist and Guido Costa Projects, Turin
pp. 174–77

Tables:
steel, plywood, acrylic paint
100 × 120 × 70 cm

## Exhibition

Curators: Anne Faucheret, Vanessa Joan Müller

Exhibition Management: Juliane Saupe

Construction Management: Johannes Diboky, Danilo Pacher

Technicians: Beni Ardolic, Frank Herberg (IT), Baari Jasarov, Mathias Kada

External Technicians: Harald Adrian, Hermann Amon, Dietmar Hochhauser, Bruno Hoffmann, Alfred Lenz

Art Handling: Scott Hayes, Johann Schoiswohl, Andreas Schweger, Stephen Zepke

Marketing: David Avazzadeh, Katharina Baumgartner, Adina Hasler, Marlene Rosenthal

Press & Communication: Stefanie Obermeir

Fundraising & Sponsoring: Maximilian Geymüller

Event Production: Gerhard Prügger

Dramaturgy: Andrea Hubin, Vanessa Joan Müller, Maximilian Steinborn, Eleanor Taylor

Education: Wolfgang Brunner, Carola Fuchs, Michaela Schmidlechner, Michael Simku, Martin Walkner

Assistant to CFO: Andrea Cevriz

Office Management: Maria Haigermoser, Vasilen Yordanov

Finances: Mira Gasparevic, Natalie Waldherr

Visitor Service: Daniel Cinkl, Osma Eltyep Ali, Kevin Manders, Christina Zowack

Kunsthalle Wien
Museumsplatz 1
1070 Vienna
Austria
www.kunsthallewien.at

Director: Nicolaus Schafhausen

CFO: Sigrid Mittersteiner

Kunsthalle Wien GmbH is the city of Vienna's institution for international art and discourse.

Stadt Wien | Kultur

Kunsthalle Wien